POINT
ZERO

POINT ZERO

CREATIVITY
WITHOUT LIMITS

Michele Cassou

JEREMY P. TARCHER/PUTNAM
a member of Penguin Putnam Inc.
New York

Most Tarcher/Putnam books are available at special quantity discounts for bulk purchase for sales promotions, premiums, fund-raising, and educational needs. Special books or book excerpts also can be created to fit specific needs. For details, write Putnam Special Markets, 375 Hudson Street, New York, NY 10014.

Jeremy P. Tarcher/Putnam
a member of
Penguin Putnam Inc.
375 Hudson Street
New York, NY 10014
www.penguinputnam.com

Library of Congress Cataloging-in-Publication Data
Cassou, Michele.
    Point zero : creativity without limits / Michele Cassou.
        p.   cm.
    ISBN 1-58542-085-9
        1. Painting—Psychology.   2. Creation (Literary, artistic, etc.).   3. Intuition.
    4. Spontaneity (Personality trait).   I. Title.
ND1140 .C38   2001   00-064834
750'.1'9—dc21

Printed in the United States of America

10   9   8   7   6   5   4   3   2   1

This book is printed on acid-free paper. ∞

TO MY SON
PHILIPPE,
WITH LOVE

Contents

This Book

I am a passionate painter. Since my early twenties, painting has filled my life with joy. But, most of all, painting has allowed me to explore the mystery of my soul. When I first discovered the power of painting, I considered myself extremely lucky because I believed I had almost missed it. I instantly wanted to share my discoveries with others. Out of my enthusiasm, I became a teacher. For almost thirty years, I have watched with delight as thousands of painters overcame their fears, broke old patterns, and tapped into that marvelous, mysterious place of creation and soul exploration.

From the very beginning of my teaching, I felt too much depended on me. I heard, much too often, "I can't paint on my own! I lose my freedom and get blocked!" I had to find a way to teach my students to rely uniquely on themselves.

In my first book, *Life, Paint and Passion,* I described the basic principles of the freedom of creation. I attempted to demystify creativity to make it available to everyone regardless of talent and technique. I explained in detail creative blocks and how they work, but I hadn't yet offered a practical way of dealing with them. Now in *Point Zero,* I am happy to present what I have discovered in the last few years—a way for *anyone to create on his or her own* and discover the joy and blessings of intuitive painting.

Point Zero presents an original method to stir up the creative potential and awaken creative passion. It describes practical ways to dissolve creative blocks and keep inspiration flowing. I believe this non-technique method brings forth uniqueness, originality, and personal style *without influencing them*. Moreover, this book stresses the depth and spiritual beauty of the intuitive force, its healing and expanding qualities.

Point Zero will give everyone who wants to create the practical means to help themselves fully through all phases of the creative process. It is based on a deep understanding of creativity and how to use self-questioning to reach Point Zero, the source of creation. The questioning process is built on the principle that creativity blossoms in a non-judgmental, non-goal approach. Stories based on real-life examples from my workshop and from my own journey as an artist illustrate this method. In *Point Zero* I present:

• the creative search as a passionate quest into life and spirit, its obstacles and astonishing discoveries.
• the concept of Point Zero, the womb of creation.
• the new non-invasive method of using self-questioning to face doubts, conflicts, or lack of inspiration.
• the three dragons that roam the land of the Creative Quest—the Dragon of Product, the Dragon of Control, and the Dragon of Meaning—and how to face them.
• the close connection and interrelation between creativity and spirit, and the power of creativity to reach into the heart and soul for healing and wisdom.

If you long to create and want to make creativity part of your life, if you are searching for what is authentic in you, I invite you to join me for the great adventure of creation—creation without limits. *No prior experience is necessary*. No need to be specially inspired or gifted. Join me in the quest for creativity through the magical teachings of *Point Zero*.

1
CREATIVITY UNLEASHED

Soulful Shelter

As a child, I loved the dizziness that came when I asked myself, "What is at the edge of the universe? What is found when all ends?" I often tried to go there to look at what happens when matter stops. My mind searched for that edge in every way possible, eager to glimpse the unknown. I wouldn't give up until I got a strange twirling feeling in my head. That sensation would tell me that I had gone as far as possible for the moment. I relished that mysterious perception. Then, without further effort, a familiar sensation of soft vertigo would arise, with the delightful feeling of having stretched my consciousness to its limit. I would arrive at that amazing place and feel totally intimate with it. With my senses outstretched to new dimensions, I recognized this as the place I came from—away from the limitation of age, body, and name, away from the narrow space allotted to me as a human. My attempts to answer my question would move me into a vastness where I knew I belonged. It felt like home.

Years later, when I let myself be fully free in my expression, I discovered that creative painting has the same effect on me. As I let my hand be guided by an inner impulse, it was moved by energies much beyond my will or comprehension. I would enter that primary place at the edge of matter, that other side of reality. Painting would slow the activity of my mind or simply short-circuit it. I was led into that great expanse where consciousness frees itself from its thoughts and knowledge. Guided by what seemed an ancient impulse, I would lose my sense of time and space. It did not matter what was being painted. My being was riding the wave, silent and soft, barely witnessing the little space where the painter was painting. Concerns about my life miraculously withered away. My familiar self seemed to do nothing as I painted. It all happened by itself. I remembered how utterly familiar was that sense of belonging to a larger reality. I had forgotten it all.

Young children go to that magical place periodically to rest and refuel, to survive in the world of knowledge where hundreds of concepts are thrown at them every day, concepts that gradually steal their capacity to reach that soulful shelter. I saw how hungry and desperate I was to meet my own self there.

I was struck with joy when I realized the underlying, meaningful aspect of the creative act, its hidden beauty and intelligence. It happened at the children's studio where, suddenly free from rules and expectations, I discovered the unending power of my intuition. There was no more encompassing path, no deeper goal for what I wanted from life. Creation would inevitably guide me to transcend my narrow boundaries, my limited thoughts, my self-identification. It would pull me away from my clinging to the know; it would break my chains and free me to explore.

From that moment on, my trust was complete. What more could I ask for? The water of creation would find its way down the mountain, over many rocks and tender soil, through rains and storms and clear weather. It would find its route, surely, in the most harmonious way, in the only possible way. I had found my guide, a guide inspired by what I could not see. Until now, my adult mind could only view one small patch of existence. Now, creation could help me transcend that limitation. Through creation, I could express myself and enjoy the delight of freedom.

Through my child eyes, I had looked at adults and wondered why they seemed to miss what was essential; why they never seemed to touch the edge of life. Back then, I was pulled between two worlds—the traditional world of things and people and the other world, vast and mysterious. Now, creativity finally cracked the shell of my own beliefs. My passion to create became the bridge between myself and the background of all things. As I reached the Point of No Return—a place of full merging with creativity—my passion turned to the search of what lies beyond the edge of the universe, and there I encountered what I had almost touched as a child. I met the spirit.

The Rose—First Step into Creation

My father liked to settle in our little den on Sundays to color black-and-white photographs of the family. Coloring photographs is a very precise and delicate task, yet he could spend hours patiently adding shades to pictures, giving them a brand-new look.

In his young years, my father had dreamed of being a painter. He loved the arts, but his parents had stressed the importance of a career to support his family-to-be. He had surrendered. "They were right," he used to say, looking thoughtfully at us, his seven children, sitting around the kitchen table. My father had become an engineer, but his dream had not died.

By the time I was four, I became aware of my father's extraordinary gift: He had the skill and the power to paint. A picture he'd painted was hanging in our entrance hall to prove it. The painting—three pastel roses on a pale blue background—was framed in gold. It was astounding.

One day, leaning against the armchair near his old, wooden desk, my father initiated me into the magic of creation. He taught me how to paint a rose. To watch the birth of something out of nothing is an experience I never forgot. It was like witnessing a miracle. It lit a fire inside me. I had always felt immense wonderment watching chicks emerge from their eggs and seeing seeds give birth to live plants, but never had I realized that I too could create, that I might have that mysterious power. With the birth of the rose, my world expanded instantly and became filled with possibilities; suddenly my dreams had places to go and my longing to create was born.

I spent the next few weeks in a sort of ecstasy, drawing and painting roses until my enthusiasm died down. Then, I went to my father and asked him to show me more of his magic secrets, but he was too busy to teach me at length. So, in my disappointment, I proceeded to learn on my own. I copied images from books and magazines. I filled coloring books and studied shapes. I worked hard and often, and started the long wait for adulthood. I knew that someday, somewhere, I would find a school, a technique, or a teacher that would show me how to make art.

While waiting, I had to find a way to prepare myself for creation. I would regularly scavenge the garbage pail next to my mother's desk and retrieve scraps of paper, cardboard, postcards, little strings, stamp endings, colored things. I made collages and constructions, even though I was always lacking most of the basic materials. I dreamed of being so rich that I could have an unending supply of tape, glue, scissors, paints, and brushes. I went to nature and gathered twigs and stones and shells and glued them together or carved them. I sculpted, varnished, and colored.

Still, I thought I needed to be taught. I had no suspicion that all I would ever need and want was inside me. That is why, years later, as soon as I could afford it, I registered at an art school in Paris.

I sat at a worktable in a classroom with twenty other students. I was given a white plaster statue of a young man's head and a dozen tools to measure and calculate proportions. Within a few minutes, the teacher had erased most of what I had done and then gave me instructions on how to use the instruments. Was this the first phase of learning? I remember searching his eyes for a spark. *Where was the passion of those who give their lives to art?* I couldn't sense any.

After just a few short weeks, I couldn't bear going to that class anymore; I was already too accustomed to my freedom. I quit and looked for other art schools in Paris. Everywhere, the same disillusion was waiting for me.

After spending a couple of years searching for the right school, I gave up painting on the advice of my last art teacher who had said, "Michele, painting is not for you. If you want to express yourself, write or do something else." I believed him and gave away my oil paints and my precious brushes. I was only in my early twenties, but I thought I had lost my lifelong dream. I became sad and depressed. I didn't know that the way had been cleared for me. I had been stripped of the idea of having any talent or being able to learn or even understand what art was. Any hope of living an artist's life had been destroyed. I had nothing left to cling to; no ready-made path I could take. Only one thing was left. I had to find my own way. I had to start from zero.

That was when I decided to find a way to work with children. If I was not talented enough to paint or to teach adults to paint, maybe I could help guide and support children, be around them, watch them create. So when I finally entered the free expression studio to watch the children paint, my eyes were free from expectations. I was able, for the first time, to see creativity floating in the air, to sense it, to touch it, to breathe it. I was so hungry for it that it filled me in an instant. My heart had found its passion, my soul its resting place. I didn't need anything from outside me. It was all in me, just as it is in every human being: the capacity, the ability, and the power to create. Nothing was missing.

A Teacher's Story

When I rediscovered my passion for painting through my work with the children, I set up a painting studio in my two-bedroom apartment in Paris and invited my friends to come and paint. Even when they had little enthusiasm, I never interfered with their work because of my great respect for the creative process. I could not forget that I had found my calling to paint among children in a place that didn't allow criticism or judgment. I had found my passion in a context of freedom and play, a place without rules and agendas. I had been left to pull entirely on my own resources to create, and it had worked like magic.

While painting with the children, I soon started holding classes and workshops in my home, determined to help painters-to-be make the same discovery: You have all you need inside to create; just follow your intuition. I knew I had no right to interfere in their paintings lest I damage their ability to find their true uniqueness. My dilemma started there. *How was I to help painters help themselves without influencing them?*

In my workshops, each held for a few days, I talked about the power of play, spontaneity, and intuition, and the principles of creativity that I had discovered through my own painting process. I developed ways to stir and stimulate creativity. Because I painted

Creative History

every day, I tested everything on myself. I came up with the funniest ideas, like having a crazy lady or man or a make-believe twin paint. (Pretending to be someone who is very free will drop self-consciousness and fear.) I introduced students to the concept of creative destruction to face intense feelings by channeling frustrated energy into strong and direct images. I expounded on the key importance of always finishing the painting, and I talked about judgments and expectations and how they damage the ability to create. I taught about listening to intuition and the necessity to respect and never destroy the work. I cautioned them again and again to *let go of product* and *embrace process.*

In my workshops, students painted for many hours every day and built a momentum of creative energy that carried them into the creative unknown. When they experienced a block or a lack of inspiration, I was there, helping them directly. They seemed to thrive under my guidance and loved to paint. Slowly, I became more involved in their process as I discovered the infinite possibilities of creativity. My teacher's intuition sharpened, and I found myself becoming more closely connected to my students' work. I looked at myself as a midwife, helping to deliver their art, or sometimes as a radar, receiving messages and sending them back to my students. I happily witnessed thousands of changes, discoveries, breakthroughs, and healings. I became an expert at dissolving creative blocks.

Unfortunately, however, few of my students painted outside my workshops. Most of them complained about not being able to find their inspiration when alone. They said they couldn't go as deep in themselves as they did in my class. The outcome of their painting seemed to become more important when nobody was there to remind them to let it go. They talked about being distracted by everything. Often, their enthusiasm for painting lasted but a short while.

My dilemma was growing. Something was not right: My teaching had made my students somewhat dependent on my interactions despite my good intentions and a method built on freedom and respect.

Why, if everyone can create, couldn't my students unblock themselves after they had experienced unblocking with my help? The question was: How could the teaching and the teacher give them the means to rely uniquely on themselves? Something had to shift. This is when I discovered that Point Zero, which had played such a huge role in my own creation, could be used as a teaching method. In a new light, I saw its amazing power and its key place in creation. This new concept gave intuitive painting a framework. Painters now could use Point Zero, a place where they could listen to their intuition at any time. Finally, they had something substantial to work with outside my workshops.

I started experimenting with Point Zero in my intensive groups with exciting results. I had students do the unblocking work I had been doing for them for so many years. It was not easy at first because they needed to have a full understanding of creativity before it could work. But soon, I was able to guide them to find and ask their own unblocking questions. They felt empowered instantly. They learned how to get out of difficult places by themselves, which could ensure a continual flow of their creation instead of being dependent on a teacher or on the volatility of inspiration.

This concept transformed my workshops. Suddenly my work as a teacher was solely to convey how creativity works and to let the students practice so they could take the method with them wherever they went. They could now explore the vast unknowns of their lives without me showing them the way anytime it became difficult.

From then on, I guided my students toward that wonderful

place. I observed that they would often ask themselves questions that didn't have the power to reach them deep inside. Their questions would talk to their minds instead of opening the door to the mysterious unknown. Like a broken compass, these questions would never find the way home to Point Zero, the womb of creation. I hammered into them that their questions had to be oriented to reach the source of creation every time; *that nothing less would do.* If they could understand Point Zero and how to build a particular question using their blocks, asking it would become simple, and it would bring back the flow of creativity automatically. What had closed the door to the creative flow would now open it. The questions had to have only one purpose: to take them back to Point Zero again and again.

I remember one week in New York a few years ago, during a workshop at the Open Center for Learning, when my new method of teaching finally fell into place and how the students felt empowered by their creativity. After only a few days, they became confident that when they were alone, they could move through the ups and downs of the creative process.

After my years of exploration, my dilemma had finally dissolved. My teaching entered the student from within to do its work at the core. Inside each painter, Point Zero was revealing itself as a source of strength and inspiration.

Two Ways
to Approach
Painting

Tell me what you plan to do with
your one wild and precious life.
MARY OLIVER

When you want to paint, you can start two ways: The first is to study the techniques pertaining to making art, such as composition, color balancing, texture, and perspective. You study until you master the skill that allows you to portray what you like. But that is not enough. You want your work to be alive and original, and you want to feel passion running through your blood. This cannot be taught. This is when the real test starts.

If you want to experience passion, you need to get your heart and soul involved. The heart needs freedom to express, respond, and invent. The fact is, you need to transcend learned techniques. Many great masters describe that place in their creative process as a turning point. Following years of work and study, they felt the urge to go beyond technique. There, they found the amazing joy of freedom and authenticity.

Trying to reach such a place, however, has a drawback. It is often a difficult challenge to reclaim freedom after years of learning and to let go of the habits and conditionings that come with it. When painters fail to find that spontaneous place, they often think that a lack of talent is responsible.

The second option is not to study at all and enter creation with innocence and freedom from the start. You discover how to be spontaneous; you develop your intuition; you follow the inspiration of your heart; you approach painting from the opposite side. Skill and technique are not the focus of the work; they will develop in time. This approach demands that you *do not focus on product*, but that you become acquainted with Point Zero, the source of creation. It liberates you from the pressures of success and failure and aims instantly toward *authenticity, personal style,* and *aliveness.* This approach requires a deep understanding of creativity and a willingness to explore. Moreover, the intuitive path affects and enhances your entire life because it demands that you respond from your whole being.

Whether you have studied painting extensively or have never painted, the approach through intuition is the same. A professional artist may find in it a renewed inspiration and fresh excitement because the intuitive world suddenly opens in the most surprising and unexpected ways. On the other hand, beginners at painting rejoice in their ability to play, experiment, and express themselves in a non-judgmental context. They may be delighted by the opportunity to play with colors and to reach feelings without outside pressures. They learn to trust what comes spontaneously and are intrigued by the unexpected images and endless combinations of forms and colors. They quickly notice the healing qualities of creativity and its potential to change their lives.

You can start creating from intuition at any point in your process, regardless of your history and goals. Whether you are a complete beginner or a professional artist, you need to unlearn what you've been taught and move beyond knowing. You must let go of your plans so the mystery can find you. When the patterns of knowing dissolve, the heart becomes engaged. Your creativity becomes stimulated and renewed through the use of Point Zero. Creative passion, then, is at hand.

2
THE
CREATIVE
QUEST

The Wondrous
Journey

Who am I?
Standing in the midst of this thought traffic.

RUMI

The quest into creativity is a journey into the heart and soul—a journey in a land filled with wonders and strange obstacles, the land of your dreamworld and its passionate and disguised wisdom. It is a place of playfulness, spontaneity, and spirit.

When you step into the Creative Quest, you enter the unlived ground of your life, the wilderness of your soul. You are there on your own, facing the creative void with nothing to rely on but yourself. No signpost. No maps. The beauty of that land untouched by others is what makes the power and magic of creation, yet it is often thought of as a desertlike country. You must get acquainted with the unknown while your mind calls for familiarity and plans. You must let your intuition guide you into the unexpected and the unimaginable.

Dragons roam the wilderness of your quest and try to stop you by any means possible, mostly tempting or threatening the limited part of your mind that deals with product and ego. Would you fight the dragons, bargain with them, or walk away? Would you let your fear of the unknown dictate your creation? Or would you fight back and find your creative power? Can you relearn to trust the intuitive and the purely spontaneous, no matter what it brings?

Dragons and doubts stand in your way, but you are given one powerful weapon, Point Zero. If you learn the art of using Point Zero, you can slay the dragons that bar your way. Every obstacle you face will reveal a hidden part of your self and will wake what was dormant or secret in you. Every challenge you meet will expand your inner world and reveal dimensions of spirit. Your playfulness, your courage to feel, and your curiosity to explore are your main allies during your Creative Quest. In your truthfulness and spontaneity, you will enter the mystery of who you are, and in the silence of your mind, you will find yourself in the heart of creation.

Point Zero

Zero
Is where the Real Fun starts
There is too much counting
Everywhere else.

HAFIZ

Point Zero is the place of all possibilities, the ground from which pure creation springs. It is a place of receptivity, with its own momentum, its own order. It is a place of *no interference,* the background of all that is. Point Zero is the time between two thoughts, the place between two breaths, a place of rest, of no movement, of silence of the mind. It is a potentially pregnant void.

You are at Point Zero when you let yourself feel, no matter what the feeling brings. Then, your feelings and perceptions mix and dance in you in a way you couldn't have imagined and can't explain. If you let your feelings be, they birth their own creation eagerly, as if they had been waiting for a long time.

If you want to discover the images that grow in your heart and soul, do not search in the drawers of the mind. To start a new painting, you need not look inside mental closets; you just need to stand

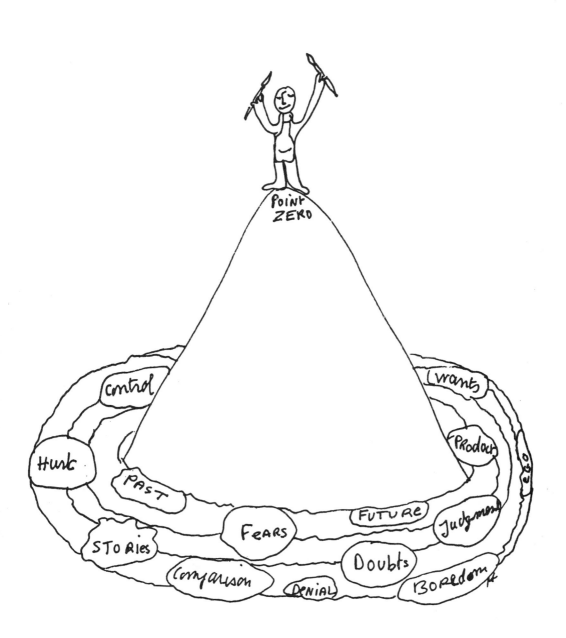

erect in the unknown, in the creative void, in the empty space, open to forms and colors. If you resist the silent space, if you want to know where you are going and what result you are going to get, you, then, would rather live with a fossil of happiness in your pocket than with the untamable flow of life in your blood.

Projection and expectation can often hypnotize you with their false offers of petty fulfillment. On the other hand, creativity has the whole universe working behind it, rushing through as the indomitable force of life like a sprout of grass breaking through the cement pathway, or a volcano erupting from the earth, or a stream of water eroding a mountain.

To reach Point Zero is to sail so far out that you cannot see land anymore with its promise of comfort and familiarity. The unexpected lives in deep waters. At Point Zero, your will surrenders and you move into the greater picture of your life. You are in a state of awakened surrender. The universal energies dig inside you, using your colors, your images, your uniqueness. Your creation carries your voice and your personal mark; it uses your life and feelings to manifest itself through you, and you experience the joy of creation because your whole being meshed with the greater spirit is at work.

Point Zero: The sharp sword of creation.

A State of Being

The most difficult part about the warriors'
way is to realize that the world is a feeling.
When one is not doing, one is feeling the world.

DON JUAN MATUS

Point Zero is a state of being. It is a place that holds no pressure, no pull, no push—a place of freedom and permission. The mind with its opinions gets out of the way. Feelings have room to be, move, interact, expand, or dissolve naturally; at Point Zero, images, shapes, and colors are given flesh and form. That state where paintings are conceived is the place you search for when you ask questions, a state of being before vested interests take over.

The mind fights creativity, always desiring to hold, possess, and use what is being created. *Pure creation rises out of being.* When encountering a block, a lack of inspiration, or trying to get out of a loop, you must look for that state of being. The mind would rather search for a clever idea or a nice product, but if you let it, you leave the land of the Creative Quest. When you find Point Zero, images manifest on your painting out of your recovered presence, your reconciliation with yourself, and your reunion with life.

The purpose of the Creative Quest is to go back again and again, against all odds and obstacles to the source of your being, to the still place, Point Zero.

To go back to Point Zero, you need to use the ego; its thoughts close the doors of intuition; its thoughts must open them. Let the ego reveal its attachments and fears, layers and layers of it. Then, destroy the power of its statements with questions. When exposed, the ego loses its control, and the door to your creativity reopens. Creativity demands that you be aware of your thoughts. Your judgments and criticisms point the way.

Why Ask
Questions?

If you do not get it from yourself,
Where will you go for it?

ZENRIN

A most effective way to deal with obstacles or lack of inspiration is by asking questions, each one designed to dissolve the particular difficulties that lie in your way. The questions stimulate your creative potential by helping break through artistic prejudices, expectations, fears, lethargy, or simply habits that stand in its path. All questions are oriented to take you back to Point Zero, the source of creation.

These custom-made questions bring you back to yourself, bring you back to the moment. It is that simple. They bring you back to who you really are. *As you fully re-enter yourself, images and colors originate out of you spontaneously.* They rise from inside and unfold in your bones as a rush of aliveness, a sudden remembrance, or a discovery because all at once you give yourself permission to feel.

Asking questions is radically different from searching for ideas. By asking, you become a hunter in the world of your inner forest, watching with great attention, sweeping the woods and fields

Afraid of the creative void

to catch the slightest movement or to hear the faintest sounds. You are alert, alive, and ready to respond. You move to a place of awakeness and playfulness, a place of surrendering to the truths that have been waiting to pass through you for all time.

Questions help you expand your sense of self and its context by pushing the boundaries of your inspiration. They put you in touch with your intuition at a deeper level, and, as a result, direct action is born.

A common problem for artists comes from a misunderstanding that says, "Let's search for something original, meaningful, deep, spiritual; let's look for interesting ideas; let's look for a message to give to society; let's visualize a result that will be art." The intention is good, but it does not work that way. To create you do not need to come up with a plan, but rather take away all plans to give natural originality, style, and wisdom a chance to manifest from your intuition.

With questions, you can dig into your creative potential as far as you want. The questions gently knock at the door of your inspiration, or bang on it, or blast it open, or anything in between so that your heart and soul can be engaged.

*Questions originate a response from all you are,
all you have been, and all you will be.*

The Power of
Questions

A voice comes to your soul
Saying lift your foot
Cross over, move into
the emptiness of question
And answer and questions.

R U M I

powerful question is one that reaches deep inside and brings
forth an unexpected response. A good question—formed using the methods you'll learn throughout these pages—takes
you back to Point Zero, to the center of your universe, ready to leap
toward the inner call.

The eye can see everything except itself. If you ask a question
with a particular interest in mind, you are like the eye straining to
see itself: you have fallen prey to the unfortunate tendency to ask
questions within the parameters of your momentary thoughts. This
is a sure way to stay blocked.

Point Zero is a place where all levels of realities and feelings
merge, where the intelligence of creation has a chance to lead you
into the unknown. When questions are not oriented toward Point

Zero, they stimulate only the mind. Your intuitive self stays unused and drags behind. When your questions are oriented toward Point Zero, they stimulate you to come back to *the place of all possibilities,* and your intuitive self brings forth unimaginable combinations of forms and colors.

As you listen to the questions, you stand in the middle of all potential, ready to respond precisely to what you need. Do not believe you have many choices when you are asking questions. Truly, your only options may be to go back to Point Zero and enter the great potential of creation or to keep turning in circles within the stories and habits that run your life.

Painting
From
Concepts

Painting
From
Emotion

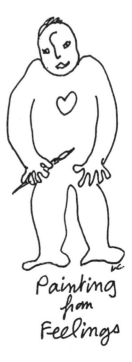

Painting
from
Feelings

How to Build
a Question

Every problem that arises in creation
holds its answer at its core.

MICHELE CASSOU

F inding the right question is an art. It requires that you understand the nature of a creative block. A creative block
happens when you think you should do something while you
are truly interested in doing something else. The block is caused by
looking in the wrong direction because of fear or prejudice, and by
striving to reach an unwanted place. *A good question must pull you
out of the fascination of thinking that you know what needs to happen* or what will make you happy. Questions bring you back to rely-
ing solely on your intuition and into the unknown and, by doing so,
dissolve the block that had stopped you.

When you understand how questions work, the right one will
fall into your lap because a true question is made out of the block.
The block is reversed and opened up to give you permission to create
from a deeper level. You must always build your question out of the
block itself, out of the judgment or fear that prevents you from creating.

You don't start a question by guessing, but by using what you already have—your criticism or reaction. Your judgments and your worries become building materials for your question. You turn them around and open them up by giving yourself space to have them. You can custom-make your question to the need of the moment.

You can start your question with, "What if I didn't have to do . . . What if it didn't matter if I did . . . What if I could let myself feel . . . What if it was okay to . . ." Just add the name of the judgment or fear and listen carefully to the answer. No more wrong choices! No more dead ends! You can flow with the natural current of your process. For example, if you think, "Why bother painting? No one will ever like what I do!" You could ask, "What if it really didn't matter if people like my painting or not?" or "What if no one will ever see my painting. What would I paint now?"

The right question unlocks your inner world at the *exact* place that prevented your creativity from flowing. Moreover, asking questions allows you to learn more about yourself by discovering your patterns of thinking and creating.

⁓⁓

"I am blocked," said Julia, a young schoolteacher from New York. She said she used to dabble in painting but had never studied art formerly. She came to the workshop to find more creativity in her life and to relieve the stress of her work.

"I really don't know what else to paint. I feel stuck," she told me.

"Have you been thinking anything about your painting?" I asked her.

"Well, I don't like very much what I have been doing. I even hate it," she answered grimly.

"What judgment did you make on your painting precisely?" I asked.

Julia's face showed increasing tension. "My painting looks as if a child painted it. It's uncoordinated, too bright, and disproportionate," she said, altogether dejected and embarrassed.

I looked at her painting, which showed an intriguing-looking head centered on the paper and two green and yellow people, with hands on their heads, at each side—a spontaneous, lively painting. Julia said she had enjoyed painting it, but now her mind had burst with pitiless judgments.

"What question could you ask yourself to unblock your inspiration?" I asked.

"What could have brought me to paint such a painting?" she asked aloud.

"Oh, no!" I said. "Trying to analyze the reason you painted it would bring you into your mind and make you think even more. You must go back to Point Zero, the womb of creation. You need to build your question out of the judgments that are stopping you right now."

"All right! What would I do next if it didn't matter if the painting was ridiculously childish and badly painted? What if . . . it really didn't matter?" she asked, with both disbelief and curiosity.

Simple questions are hard to hear because the mind discards them quickly as too naïve. But Julia must have heard its impact because something in her clicked. She suddenly turned inward, took a deep breath, and the beginning of a smile reached her lips.

"I could paint a red tree, purple vines wrapping around the people, and pink sunrays," she said in one breath, images rushing to her with no thought. She turned back to her painting, moved by the joyful play of creation. She had just discovered a crack between the narrow boundaries of her judgments, squeezed through, and freed herself.

Julia's thoughts had stopped her. The idea of painting childish images had killed her enthusiasm.

"I will know now what to do if this happens again. It's simple!" she marveled, her eyes looking far into a possible future filled with playful creativity for her and her art-hungry students.

Painters slide again and again into their critical mind, succumbing to their fears and judgments. Questions get them out, time after time, until their creative muscles are so strong that judgments and fears lose the power to stop them.

Dragons

The land of the Creative Quest is filled with many dragons, each especially designed by your own mind to make you fall prey to various prejudices or fears. These dragons represent the parts of you that resist change and exploration. The dragons watch your work, ready to spring and act at the slightest opportunity. Quick as lightning, they sometimes take over before they can be spotted. They feed on criticisms, comparison, and evaluation. Three main dragons roam the land. They are:

The Dragon of Product: This dragon fights your spontaneity because it loves esthetics. It wants you to plan exactly how your finished painting will look. It gorges itself on the ideas of success and failure. It generates attachment and expectations, taking your freedom away.

The Dragon of Control: This dragon guards the doors of the unknown by using fear to stop true exploration. It feeds on your lack of trust in your spontaneity and fear of changes and tries to convince you that you must be in control of your creation at all times.

The Dragon of Meaning: This dragon fights your intuition by demanding interpretation and resolution at every move. It wants you to analyze your creation and assign meaning to everything you paint. It prevents you from exploring your feelings at deeper levels and entering the mystery of your life.

The Three Dragons

3
THE DRAGON
OF PRODUCT

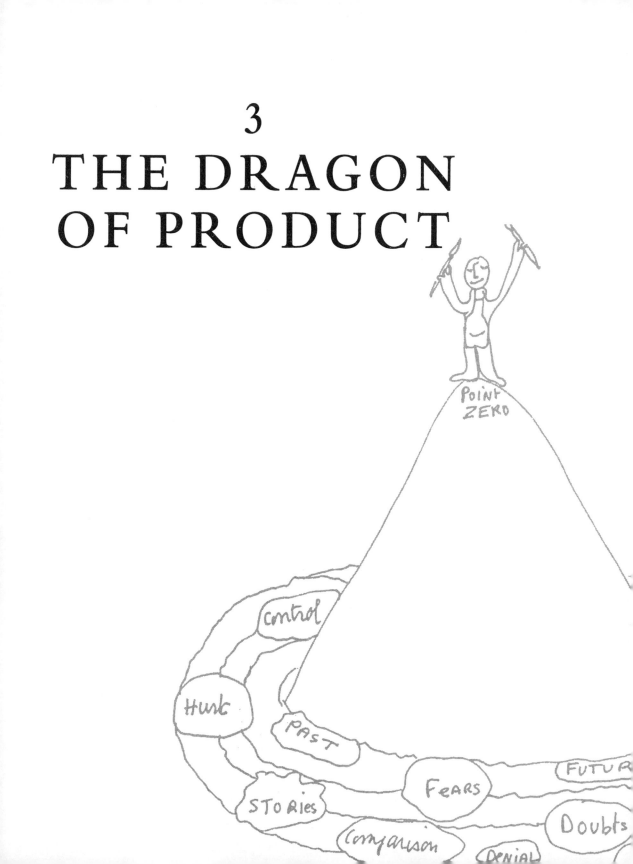

I Can't Paint!

*The more skill you have
the further you are
from what your deepest love wants.*

RUMI

The mind is convinced that it needs to know, that it needs instruction, skill, or talent to paint something that looks like what it is meant to represent. It is very old, inherited conditioning and is the most common and most pervasive barrier to the creative process. You can fight the Dragon of Product for days and weeks and years and become tense, frustrated, discouraged, and ready to give up. The belief that you do not know how to paint destroys enthusiasm and spontaneity and prevents the flowering of intuition.

When you go for what you think may look good instead of what needs to be painted, you ignore your intuition. As a result, your painting looks stiff, awkward, and without life. You fix it and rework it endlessly, never reaching the desired effect. You become frustrated and overwhelmed. Creativity has fired back by generating blocks.

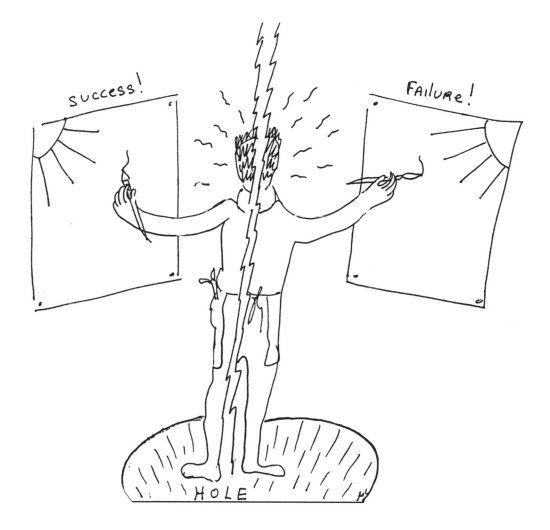

Painters love the idea of spontaneity and hope to have instant skill appear along with it. *Technique and the ability to paint gradually and spontaneously develop on their own.* When the images look childish or out of proportion, it's a good sign, proof of the truthfulness and directness of the painter.

When feelings are allowed to express themselves, images find their appropriate form and substance. The parts of the painting that you are tempted to judge are often the most authentic and genuine because in it, all has been invented. They may seem to clash when put against an expected blueprint, but they carry the birth of the uniqueness of your personal style. And it doesn't matter how accurate they are because liveliness and presence inhabit them.

The mind needs to unhook from the idea of a well-painted image. When spontaneity develops and intuition is practiced, the way you look at your paintings changes, first slowly, then drastically. You learn to look at the images and paintings through the heart. What is pure and authentic is finally seen.

♋

George, a middle-aged man with a lifelong passion for creativity, joined the workshop. He had no art training of any kind. He had painted orange and green mountains bordered with hot lights, a blue sky, and a red sun with carmine rays.

"I don't know what else to do!" he said, discouraged.

"What question could you ask to find out what's next?" I asked him.

"I can't think of anything!" George exclaimed.

"You must have some judgment or thoughts stopping you. What are they?"

He looked inside, and an ironic smile spread across his face. "I don't want to ruin what I have done," he admitted, disturbed by the absurdity of such concern for what he thought was a worthless painting. His frustration came out: "I can't paint images! Michele, you don't understand. I cannot get the product that I want. It does not come out. The paintbrush paints and does what it wants, not me. I am not with it. I cannot give my painting the form I want. I cannot paint! I need to *know how* first!"

"The Dragon of Product has got hold of you! You must find out what is it that you would do if you were free of the thought that you can't paint? Can you build a question out of your judgments?"

"I could put a black square in the left bottom corner," he said, disheartened.

"Why don't you ask your question aloud. Keep in mind that you need to go back to Point Zero."

"What could I paint if I was not afraid to ruin my painting and didn't let myself be stopped by the certainty of not knowing how to paint my images?" he asked grimly, but he listened. All of a sudden, the space around him seemed to expand. "On the right corner, I could paint an odd face," he said with a weak spark in his eyes.

"Anything else?" I asked, encouraging the flow.

"A little man, climbing the mountain . . . other men could be all over!" he said, suddenly playful, spontaneous images flowing from inside. They had enough life in them to make him forget about his lack of skill. George became so curious about doing them that he didn't take time to worry. Play, the first step of creation, had pulled him into his dreamland.

Within a few minutes, several little men had appeared on the mountains and on the right of them, another man, much bigger with blue pants, a red shirt, and mysterious green balls surrounding him.

A little later that afternoon, George turned toward me, looked thoughtfully into my eyes, and pointed to his spontaneous images. "It's perfect," he said.

George had chipped away a piece of that stubborn desire for technique. A fresh stream of liveliness and freedom had just been released, and he knew it. He had won his first battle with the Dragon of Product.

Judgments point out to you where you are closing the door to your creativity.

Find Your Freedom

The one who keeps her heart awake,
Though the eye of her head may sleep
Her heart will open a hundred eyes.

RUMI

o create from intuition, you need to free yourself from the demands and expectations of product. These pressures strangle your potential to create and prevent true enjoyment and passion. Inside you lives the worst judge and the most tyrannical ideas of what you should do and how your finished product should look.

The amount of freedom you experience is always a function of how much *permission* you give yourself. If your freedom has disappeared, you must find the thief who lives inside you as long as you put up with it. When you learn to recognize that compromising presence, you destroy its ability to steal your freedom. In fact, when the thief discovers that it cannot steal from you anymore, it leaves on its own accord. The thief is your mind, burdened with ideas of good and bad, success and failure. The mind dreads Point Zero. The

Attachment to Product

mind cannot survive in that space. Point Zero consumes its judgment and defeats its control over the outcome, taking away its power.

To find your freedom, you need to become aware of that part of you that snatches your spontaneous tendencies and replaces them with secondhand ideas, keeping you at bay, as far as possible from Point Zero. The questions you ask to find a state of creative flow must be directly oriented to find which influences are not yours so you can stop them. The questions must free you to use feelings and intimations spontaneously. The questions must allow you to bypass the *should* and the *have to* and finally be on your own, free to roam, in your own land.

❧

Tania, a woman in her thirties with dark eyes shining in a thin, angular face, had painted a trio of golden-brown horses riding in a dazzling sunset of lavender and fire tones. Large, deep-green leaves moved like shadows in the foreground. Two white spots on the paper were left undone, one on the bottom right corner and a smaller one on the upper left.

"Do I have to fill the white spaces for the painting to be complete?" she asked me. "I have felt pretty good painting. I was absorbed, involved, but now I'm wondering about the white places. I don't know what to do there. Do I have to paint them? Is it a feeling? Is it intuition?"

"What question could you ask yourself to find out?" I asked her. "It is important that you learn to answer every question you have by yourself."

"Why don't I want to paint the white?" she attempted.

"Oh, no!" I said. "You don't need to analyze your confusion. What you need is to give yourself full permission to do it or not, and truly feel, so your intuition can answer your question."

"A question could be, 'What would I do next if I *didn't have to* paint the white spaces and could do anything I wanted?'" she said.

"Yes!" I said. "This question opens permission within yourself."

"I think I'd like to simply fill the white spaces with lavender color. Yes! I would like to do that," she said matter-of-factly, as if the reason for her question had suddenly vanished. And it had, because the instant the feeling awakens, the mind has no more choice.

Tania had decided to put colors in the white spaces, not because it was expected or because it was right or wrong, but simply because she felt it. The permission she had given herself to do it or not allowed her to sense her true need. There is no rule in creativity—no special technique to arrive at a finished product—because in it there are no points of comparison and no possible tracks to follow. Every moment, every place in creation is unique. Intuition knows how to respond to the slightest need. Questions are the guides.

Remember, you are not painting a picture,
you are just painting!

Intuition Is Always
on Your Side

The bluebird carries the sky on his back.
HENRY DAVID THOREAU

The Dragon of Product challenges you to worry about and take seriously every little turn in your process. If you let yourself be present and feel, if you let your intuition take over, the dragon loses the fight. So *the dragon's strategy is to distract you from yourself.* It impresses upon you that it is up to you to search your mind for the next step; that you should look for images and shapes that match what you have already painted in order to complete your painting. It certainly does not want you to see that the most powerful thing you can do is get out of the way and let forms and colors happen naturally and spontaneously at their own rhythm.

◌◌

Dora, a tall, slender blond woman with a twinkle in her eye, was a social worker who wanted to integrate painting expression in her work. She had just painted herself with her chest wide open and an exotic blue bird flying out—a bird with a long, curved, multicolored tail.

"I am quite attached to that bird," she warned me. "I love the way it came out and I loved painting it! I don't want to mess it up. But now, I am wondering what to paint around it. I have thought a lot about it, and all of a sudden, I went dead blank."

"What question do you need to ask to lift you from all this thinking?" I asked her.

"I need to stop focusing on the bird, but I do not know how to do it," she added.

"You have been on a one-track search and seem to have exhausted possibilities. You have an agenda of where and how to paint next, and you've lost your freedom. The Dragon of Product has got hold of you and is now controlling your thoughts and desires. Your own attachment to your painting is keeping you prisoner. How can you fight back?"

"Okay," she said, "I could explore around the little head down there." She motioned to a small pale face barely visible on the bottom right.

"No! That would be deciding where to go! You need to have your *intuition* guide you, not your mind. At this point your needs are a mystery to you. You must go back to not knowing to discover them. Go back to Point Zero."

"Okay," she said, trying to understand. "I could ask what could come from behind the shoulder."

"No, this won't work either," I told her. "It's the same kind of question. Any answer to that question would keep you stuck. You need a more general question, one that would bring you to Point Zero, one that would take you to the very top of the mountain of your life with a 360-degree panoramic outlook. Then by looking all around, by being open to anything, you will notice what is calling you because it will *stand out* on its own. For instance, a question that might help could be 'What would I do if anything could appear in the painting all at once from anywhere?'"

And the question did hit home because Dora instantly perked up. "I would paint hands on her cheek . . . large man hands, ocher in color."

"Yes," I said, with a smile, "this came from a vast space! You see, what needed to appear did not come where you were expecting it. The Dragon of Product was trying to have you protect what you had done by dictating where to paint next. You need to trust that if your intuition guided you and gave you something you like, it is not going to drop you and make you ruin everything. Intuition is always on your side."

"The energy is back," she said, amazed at how simple it could be, "and I even like my painting better now!"

The fear of ruining your painting means that you have not completely surrendered to your intuition.

Do I Need a Plan?

Live in the nowhere that you came from
Even though you have an address here.

RUMI

*C*reation happens in the moment. Every trace of color, every shape, gives birth to the next one. If you follow your intuition, the current of your inspiration carries you into the unexpected liveliness of the dreamland, into the mystery of your inner self. Nothing is known in advance. The finished product is not set in advance. You discover as you go, step by step. *Planning would be creating in the past.* It would miss the adventure of creation with its unending surprises and revelations. No need to worry about what is next. The image-maker does not make plans and does not compose. Creation follows natural rhythms, like waves. Creative currents build up and explode and rebuild endlessly following larger cycles. The end is always a beginning. The image-maker responds to the totality of feelings and perceptions. It moves within the context of the life and spirit. Planning would be traveling in the context of the known mind only.

◠◠

Martin, a man in his thirties with inquiring blue eyes, came to the workshop. He had not painted since childhood. He spent two days getting acquainted with this new medium. The third day, a wave of spontaneity swept through him as he started a new painting. Two big flesh-tone hands reached from each side of the painting as if to grab something in the middle.

He called me over to him. "I am wondering if it is okay to plan the whole succession of images for the entire afternoon. I can practically see the finished painting! I first saw two big hands. Then I saw a large nose and eyes and then I saw the body of a woman. Should I go ahead and paint them, or should I follow the intuition of the moment?"

Planning

"Did the images come to you spontaneously?" I asked.

"Yes, they surprised me and came quite quickly."

"You could ask yourself: what could I paint if I didn't have to follow a plan?" I suggested. *Point Zero will bring what has most energy at each moment."*

"The woman!" he replied instantly.

"You got your answer. Paint the woman and let go of everything else. As you paint the woman, feelings will move in you and the images you thought of may change, losing interest for you or becoming more pressing. If some images are important, they will come back when the time is ripe. No need to burden yourself with a plan you may not likely follow."

Martin painted the woman's body. His face softened. When he turned to look at me, I asked, "Did your painting evolve the way you thought it would at the beginning?"

"You see that little green chair in the corner?" he asked, pointing to the right corner of his painting. "It appeared with three green legs and one brown. I don't know where that came from or what it means!" he said, marveling at the mystery. "Nothing happened as I first saw it and not in the succession I imagined. By the time I was there, I was gone. I was somewhere else." And without taking another moment, he went back to paint some green vines adorning the woman's body.

*Your best weapon against any set pattern
is your spontaneity.*

You Don't Need
a Reason

*Y*ou never need a reason to paint something. An image that has a reason to be painted comes from the mind. The mind pulls images from its storage of memories or conditionings, what it thinks is beautiful, interesting, or meaningful. It wants to know where the painting is going and how it will end. The product is its goal.

On the other hand, intuition is free, never tied to a reason; its outcome is mysterious and unexpected. You don't even need to work at it. *Creation is a response; it is not something you have to make.* You only deliver colors and shapes that the great postman of creation entrusts you to carry. No need to struggle and guess where to take them and how. They come with their package fully addressed. Don't take on extra work!

ᦉᦉ

Rose had four years of art school. On the day she arrived at my workshop, she said that she could not paint anymore. She had come to the point of dreading to create: She kept starting paintings but could never finish them because she would lose interest in them. She was getting very frustrated and discouraged.

In the workshop, Rose had painted a soft-purple dancing woman with high black boots. An emerald river flowed through the middle of the painting between dark mysterious grounds; one exotic tree stood there, a little person sitting against it.

"I don't know what to do," she said, pointing to the upper part. "I don't want to paint the sky blue. It's too boring. Should I do something else instead, or should I just paint it pink?"

"When you think you have a choice to make, what can you do to find out what you really need to do?" I asked.

"I could ask a question, I guess. Should I paint the sky pink?"

"Oh, no! You need to open the space for yourself; you need to come back to Point Zero so the creative energy can pass through you and guide you. The answer is its job, not yours. Try again."

"What if I could paint anything anywhere, what would I do?" she asked herself. Her answer came too quickly. She didn't take the time to really listen. "I would paint a little creature in the tree because the tree is so lively, so it needs something lively in it!"

"Since when do you need a reason to paint something?" I asked. "Intuition is not reasonable. The entire universe is its reason!"

"In my art school," Rose started to explain, "it was pounded into my head that every little stroke of paint should have a reason, whether meaning or looks. I can't stop it anymore!"

"Do you think it is possible to know more and better than your creative intuition?" I asked her. "*To create is to move in the unknown.* This is why creation is so alive and interesting! It looks like the Dragon of Product has taken over and is barring your way to the land of your Creative Quest."

"I don't want it to take over, but I don't know how to stop it," she said.

"What question could you ask yourself to bring you back to a more spontaneous place, back to your Creative Quest?"

"If I didn't need to have a reason to do something, what would I do?" she asked quickly, and that is when the shift happened: "I would put fish in the river and sparks flying in the sky," she said, surprising herself with a newfound freedom.

A half-hour later, I went back to see her.

"This is freedom!" Rose exclaimed, as if a great discovery had just happened.

"That feeling is what will keep you creating; what will generate your passion," I told her, as I watched her paint a fluorescent-red rose between the fancy black boots.

If what you paint has a reason, it is not intuitive.

The Spontaneous Development of Technique

When I started to paint intuitively, I was determined to explore my freedom to its limits. I painted every day, long hours. I painted bold, primitive, and often childlike paintings. I used plain colors and painted simple details. I loved moving fast because I was years behind in my creativity. My freedom was sacred to me, and I wouldn't hear anything about technique, composition, or esthetics. I kept my studio door well-locked against the Dragon of Product. I practiced sensing my intuition and letting it create.

I discovered the physical reality of my creative energy. I observed and studied it; the creative force was definitively tangible. For instance, I noticed that if I ate just before painting, I could not find it as well inside of me and I would miss it terribly. I would then stay on the surface of my creativity, not knowing any other way to reach in. Slowly, I found out *how* and *where* to find my intuition. I learned to use it in the best way possible. The fire of creative passion burst in me. I couldn't get enough of painting. It was never hard to start painting, only to stop.

My paintings were raw and done quickly, but as time went on, I painted more and more details on them, mostly lines and dots. (See painting no. 9.) One day, to my surprise, the lines on the paintings began blurring slightly into one another. It happened spontaneously, and I just watched the transition. Within a couple of weeks, my brush would melt the colors into one another, giving my paintings a new look. This new way of painting, this spontaneous "technique" expanded immensely my capacity to paint more subtle and precise images. Without effort or study, the way I painted had organically evolved to give me more options. *When I needed the technique, it had suddenly appeared.* The intelligence of creation was at work.

The same sort of evolution happened when I began painting images. When I started, I painted them in the strangest forms. As time went on, they miraculously found their true shapes and proportions, but only when I was inwardly ready. My technique developed though I never forced my images to conform or look a certain way.

Never showing my paintings to others helped because I was always free to follow my intuition's slightest hints without having to worry about what people would think of what I had produced. I felt at peace with the idea of not showing my work to anyone. If that were the price of my creativity, I wouldn't argue. This trade-off for my freedom was too life-sustaining to be ignored. I still thought of myself as an artist, but a secret one.

A year or two later, unusual circumstances brought a professional artist to see my work. He was genuinely shocked. "How can you put purple against orange? That is simply not done!" He sounded as if he were personally offended. I smiled and said nothing in reply, but six months later, I noticed a sudden discomfort while I was painting. Then I realized that I was again in the process of putting orange against purple. I was stunned. Despite my better knowledge, my unconscious had stored that man's comment, it had been incarnated as a Dragon of Product, and now it was attacking my freedom! At that moment, I understood how vulnerable I was to criticism. For six months, that small judgment had lodged in me, eating a piece of my freedom. Unnoticed, my mind had given authority to that comment, transforming it into an esthetic rule, thus limiting my ability to fully explore spontaneous technique and harmony. From then on, I was very careful to protect myself until my creative muscle had become so strong that my mind wouldn't react. I wondered how much conditioning I still had to undo to find true freedom.

Spontaneous technique evolves as we practice listening to intuition. But this is only part of the journey. Intuitive painting is an inner discipline, a way of life, a meditation.

Concepts Are
Empty Skins

Only the unexpected is real.
NISARGADATA MAHARAJ

Images are alive. Concepts are empty skins. The moment you focus on an abstraction, you have not only rejected your image-maker and its power of invention, but you have been swallowed by a concept. Trying to transform a concept into an image, into a finished product, is not a creative action. It is a mental exercise, a manipulation, like dreaming of many possible journeys while looking at a map instead of hitting the road, ready for adventure.

Under the layers of thoughts, images are constantly being born and wait for delivery. If you let yourself respond to images, not to words, images enter your creation freely and easily. They procreate and multiply, throwing their seeds to the wind until infinity. You will delight in watching them grow and reveal themselves.

Natasha had just finished painting a woman and a man embracing in the middle of a dense, colorful jungle. "I don't know what to do next," she told me with a pathetic look.

"Can you ask yourself a question to find out?" I asked.

"What would I paint if I didn't censor anything?" she asked herself. A moment passed. "Up there . . . God!" she exclaimed, surprised by her own inspiration.

"What does God look like?" I asked.

"I have no idea. I couldn't possibly imagine. . . ." She became silent for a while, thinking hard. "I could paint Him as a round, big shape, pastel pink and yellow," she said.

"If you do not attempt to translate the concept of God into an abstract shape, what would come naturally to you?" I asked.

Natasha looked shy and embarrassed. "Oh, I see God as an old man with a long white beard! But that's ridiculous, I know. Something I got from Sunday school!"

"Let's go one step further," I said. "Go deep inside, find Point Zero, and let the image of God rise. It is obviously there, *looking for its way out*. What question could you ask if you use your block to build it?"

Again Natasha focused on the area above the jungle of trees in her painting.

"What would I do if God could have any shape at all and I was not afraid to be soupy?" she asked herself, with a half-smile playing on her lips. The answer came. "I see a blue face, a spiritlike face, somewhat transparent with golden rays radiating into the sky. Oh, yes!" she said with the voice of someone who had just received a gift.

Don't try to paint your feelings—feel and paint.

A Good Question
Speaks to the Heart

*E*ven if you know that there are no rules when it comes to painting from your intuition, that there is nothing that you *have to* do, you might still unintentionally make up new ones. Who says that you should paint the next empty space? Who says that you need to come up with ideas to fill the entire painting? Or the opposite? The mind—the Dragon of Product—incessantly demands instruction, parameters, anything with a direction so it won't have to surrender to intuition.

You never need to stare at a blank space on your painting and wonder what to do there, trying to coerce something that is not ripe in a place that is not ready to be painted. When the time comes, it will be there. In the meantime, *you need to respond to the whole painting, not to a particular spot, empty or not.* By bringing you back to the state of all possibilities, Point Zero will bring you what you need. Let your images and colors unfold at their own rhythm. It is not your job to choose what is next, but to respond from your heart.

☙

Janine painted quite often a few years earlier but had not touched a brush in a year. A young woman in her thirties, intelligent and dedicated, she had come to the workshop to reconnect with her creative passion. She had painted a woman in a sitting position holding an adolescent girl in her extended arms. Both figures had been painted with a thousand multicolored, vibrant strokes.

She called me over to her. "I am not sure what to paint there," she said, pointing to the right corner of her painting. I thought of a blue clown head or a bird, up there among clouds." She hesitated. "I don't know if I want to paint the head or the bird. I feel about the same for both."

"What question could you ask yourself to find out?" I said.

"Which one do I want to do more?" she asked herself. Still, she had no clue. Frustrated, she said, "Then, I don't know what else to ask!"

"What about going back to Point Zero? Your question asked your mind for its opinion. Don't speak to your dragons. *A good question speaks to the heart,*" I told her.

"How do I do it?" she asked curiously.

"You have to find what stopped you first. You just told me that you thought you *should* fill that corner. That type of pressure would most likely create a block every time. You think you have to go there simply because logically it seems to need it. Creation does not move through logic. You are trying to force yourself to come up with a consistent idea to fill that space, and your heart rebels. Let go of your idea of product, of what you think you should do, and let yourself be vulnerable. Let your heart melt."

"What would I paint if I could let myself *feel anything,* if I could be wide open, and *especially* if I didn't have to paint in the right corner?" she asked herself, and there was an instant change in her behavior. "Oh! I could paint green vines growing up from the woman's chest and gently enveloping the child—and yellow flowers blooming on them!" she exclaimed joyfully. "Yes! I am going to do that."

"Interesting," I said. "You want to paint something that is different from your two choices, and it won't even fill your empty corner! Now you can see the importance of going to Point Zero to find the next thing. You were caught in a tunnel with only two options that really didn't interest you much. Point Zero brought you back to your heart and gave you what you need."

The mind acts reasonably.
Intuition is wild and unpredictable.

On Trying to Make
Your Painting
Look Alive

We are a smart species. We know when something is not alive. We may buy artificial flowers occasionally, but we are not fooled. However, as strange as it seems, when artists paint, they tend to forget that *life cannot be infused into the canvas by manipulating colors and shapes.* They forget that the breath of life arises spontaneously only when the work is done from the heart and soul, in humility and surrender.

Artists struggle to paint the appearance of life, confusing it with aliveness itself. They study all sorts of techniques to perfect the illusion and come up with a finished product that has a life of its own. The belief that it can be done is a big trap that can swallow them whole—body, mind, canvas, paints, and brushes. Discouraged artists think a lack of talent and skill is responsible for such failure, unaware that if they had been able to succeed in the illusion, they would have lost the chance to become real and truthful in their art.

Any time you try to cheat the true spirit of creation, you fall back into the same mushy soup of superficiality and frustration—and that is excellent. Learn to swim out of it.

The great gift of creativity is that it does not let you mimic life in a satisfactory way. It forces you to really explore the truly vibrant within you.

Tired and
Bored

If you are lugging a heavy bag,
Don't fail to look inside it
To see whether what is inside
Is bitter or sweet.

RUMI

When the Dragon of Product has got hold of you, boredom and tiredness inevitably arise. The fact is simple: The dragon leads you to paint what you are not truly interested in. The dragon makes you think of the finished product; *what you think you should do* is fighting with *what you want to do.* You lose energy, you become exhausted or discouraged, your intuition withdraws.

It is hard to keep painting. You indulge in thinking how good it will be to breathe some fresh air or do some errands or go to a movie. Your intuition is actively giving you a message. Can you read it? The message is clear: *Stop doing what you are doing now! You have lost your freedom.*

The intelligence that passes through creativity is at work, trying to inform you of other possibilities. It refuses to cooperate with your lack of involvement, your denial, or just your lack of presence. You have taken a side road and have gotten lost. Your creative compass is off. You need to come back to yourself and assess the situation. The fact is, you are not painting what you need to paint at that moment, and are going *further* and *further* from yourself; you are merely following an old blueprint and filling in the blanks. You have gone on mechanical. It does not matter why. The point is, you left your creative stream and you need to go back as soon as possible or you will encounter a creative block. Observe the process that leads to boredom and tiredness, and respond. It is time to give yourself permission to be free again, time to go back to Point Zero.

The appearance of boredom and tiredness is a sign that you are not listening to your intuition.

Painting
Your Body

When I started painting from intuition, I instantly loved painting bodies. I gave myself the freedom to paint them any way I felt like—body-shape, size, proportion, extra parts. I would go to extremes and bend or twist or expand them. It was a thrill after having taken life-drawing classes and struggling so hard to be accurate and original, trying to produce what was expected. I remember the day I painted the sexual part of a body for the first time—a little blue hole in the pubic area. I was astonished at how far the experience went inside me. At the time, I painted and slept in the same room and spent the entire night looking at my painting in the moonlight—a long woman's full body in lavender tones standing against a simple rose background. I felt as if I had just been initiated into a new life.

Whether you have studied painting or not, you need to approach painting your body with vulnerability and openness. Doing a painting of your body can be scary if you think you have to portray a physical or emotional resemblance. You must remember that you paint to give form to the invisible and to depict attributes beyond the concrete appearance. You paint to give form to what is hiding inside you and to let your dreamworld unfold. To find freedom, you must push aside what you learned about life-drawing and start from

Point Zero. Proportion, texture, shadow, and colors should obey your spontaneous intuition. Intuitive painting is never a translation or a photographic reproduction. Spending time trying to reproduce the perfect idea of your body would be like fussing over wrapping paper and never opening the package.

Painting your body is an opportunity to feel. The way you experience your body changes constantly with your passing moods and feelings. When feelings meet the creative force, the images take on shapes and colors that may not have much to do with your expectations. Express them without restraint. Forget about perspective and proportions. Feel the joy of unending possibilities. What you paint does not have to make sense.

To paint your body, you don't need to think about how you feel. Your intuitive sense already knows that. You need only to let feelings and sensations pass through you without manipulating them.

Are your feet so big that they cover the whole floor? Or maybe so tiny that you can barely touch the ground? Maybe you do not even have feet right now. Not having feet is a very special feeling, too, and sometimes feet are simply not there. What about the texture of your skin? Is it smooth, scaly, furry, bumpy? Has it holes in it; is it different colors? The question is, can you let yourself enjoy the incredible ingeniousness of creativity that finds ways to express the feelings of the moment, no matter how mysterious or strange?

You don't need to describe your body to yourself, but you must keep in mind that you are painting a body so you won't find yourself transforming it into a different image. (You must always keep the image your intuition gave you. If not, intuition will stop working for you.)

When you let yourself sense, the body paints itself spontaneously. If one part of your painted body reaches the edge of your

painting and does not fit in, it is no accident or miscalculation. Remember that the creative flow depicts feelings and sensations, not physiological facts. *Invent* and *reinvent* your body, as you let your brush trace the outline. Let yourself be surprised; enjoy the suspense.

❦

Jane had the flu. She painted her body pale blue and in perfect proportion. She looked exhausted and quite miserable.

"How do you really feel at this moment?" I inquired.

"I feel all swollen, heavy like a ton. I've got a stiff back and a sore throat," she admitted grimly.

"How would you paint your body if you let yourself feel? Don't attempt to translate your sensations into words. Let them come directly from Point Zero. Ask yourself questions," I suggested.

"Okay, I'll try," she agreed, and I went off to help another student.

When I returned, Jane was painting a heavy, dark-green woman with black spikes coming out of her crimson throat and a red, swollen head with electric-orange hair. She seemed totally involved in her creation. I marveled at how much healthier Jane suddenly looked.

*You have a million body images within your
own feeling-body. Let them express themselves!
Don't be concerned by the extremes they might go for.
Delight in them.*

The Wax Museum
of Your Mind

Taking a new step, uttering a new word
Is what people fear most.

FYODOR DOSTOEVSKI

The mind is full of expectations, beliefs, and desires. The ego strives to get what it wants and clings to it rather than move with the fluidity of creation. Every desire for product builds a scene in the wax museum of the mind. You need only to visit this museum to see what could be painted when you are in control. All is there, in the expression of the wax figures and their stories. But as long as you believe there is life in the wax, you are going to spend time there, reproducing what you see. When you finally realize that the wax is inert, you step out of that stuffy place and meet the lively world of your creation. You learn to enjoy the unexpected and its unborn potential. You are drawn to the mystery. You listen to the endlessly new voice of creation.

Watch your mind when it grabs the concept of what you think you should paint, when it dresses it up, puts costumes on it, and hopes it's alive. These concepts belong in the wax museum. They are clothed projections, artificial things, stereotypes. They will never replace a fresh and mysterious painting no matter how long you work on it. When you let yourself feel, images jump out, and when they come out, you don't need to dress them up.

Marguerite had painted a large painting of a woman in flesh tones. "I feel something needs to be painted around the hands, but I can't find what it is," she told me.

"Don't look there! Don't search there!" I insisted. "By forcing an area to be painted, you call on your inner repertory. At this moment, the gate to your creative energy lies somewhere else. Open the big gate, not the door to your wax museum. The big gate is the unknown, where images and colors come at their own time, in their own way, and in their own place. Stop grabbing what you think might be there. Go back to Point Zero, the ground of your creativity; go toward the obvious, the easy. They are places where what needs to come next is evident. No need to force anything. Painting is not about adding. It grows like a garden. Its next move is born from what is already there. It is on its way. Trust the timing; go where it's ripe. *There is always one place in a painting that is ready at each moment;* find it."

Marguerite suddenly looked thoughtful. "What would I paint next if I didn't have to find something around the hands? What could I do . . . if it could be anywhere else . . . if it could be anything?"

Her intuition moved in, and she let go of product. "I see a little boy in the back!" she exclaimed, taken aback. "I am going to paint him!" And she began to trace the child's face, her heart awakening to a secret place.

*Ask yourself what will happen if you stop
deciding if this is better than that.*

Point of Contact

hen you paint, you never need to plan the finished product or make sure your ground is covered, not even for a single image. Every image unfolds in its own way. Don't let the Dragon of Product paint it for you with its logic, reasons, and lack of liveliness. Start at the point of contact and move from there. Enjoy and invent, moment to moment. Be adventurous. Jump in.

When images are born, they are born in a unique fashion and need to develop from a precise place. *The birthplace of an image is its place of energy.* For instance, if you want to paint a body, you first start where the feeling is the strongest, the hand, the head, the stomach. The place of energy is where you start to paint the image. The same image might grow from a different place at various times. The birth of truly felt images never follows patterns. A different order of things is in motion. You must respond from that place if you want to feel the real thrill of creation. You must ride the current of your inspiration and forget the possible outcome.

Roger, a young European art-school student, had come to my workshop to release his high standards of accomplishment and recover the joy of painting he had felt as a child.

"I painted a snake biting the throat of that man, but now that it is done it looks mild, almost nice. The snake could be giving him a kiss. It's not what I tried to do," he told me.

"When you have a strong feeling about doing something, you must start at the point of contact, the place where the feeling is born, where the energy is running strong. Go there. Start at the biting place, at the tip of the teeth. Forget about the rest of the snake. Your intuition will guide you," I encouraged.

"Are you saying that I don't need to think of the whole snake and the whole painting in advance? Are you telling me that I should trust that after I finish the teeth, I will know what to do to finish the snake?" he asked.

"That's right!" I answered. "Your intuition gave you the image of the teeth, knowing there is a whole snake attached to it. It has already prepared a place for it. It is not a biological birth. We could say that your snake is born out of its teeth. You are in the dream-world, remember. You were visualizing, preparing and planning, you were birthing a snake in your head. It's not a good way to approach creation. No life there, just rendering of ideas. It's work. You would be missing the best part. In other words, go where the feeling is and don't worry about the future!"

Roger returned to his painting and started another snake or rather started to paint snake's teeth. He was grinning at the audacity of his gesture and at the rush of freedom that suddenly invaded his body.

Make your intuition happy! Listen to it by following the energy, not the idea of a product!

Inside the Heartbeat
of Creation

I waited for spring recess, counting the days. The children would be off from school, and the painting studio would be closed. It would be deliciously empty. I would go in.

I had a project. My dream had become more and more pressing. I wanted to paint a painting as big as the studio, a painting that would cover the four walls from floor to ceiling and the door. I longed to be surrounded by my own creation, to be totally absorbed, to melt in it. I wanted to erase the line that separates creator and creation.

The studio, a small rectangular room maybe ten by twenty feet, has all its walls covered by soft boards where children pin up their papers. The room has been multicolored by hundreds of painters whose brushes swept past the borders of their paintings, leaving traces of colors. The studio has no windows, expect for one very small opening against the ceiling. It has no door, either, or so it seems: the door, which is covered just like the walls, disappears when it is closed. It is a sacred space. I was shocked one day to discover that fifteen years earlier this room had been a meat freezer in the back of a butcher shop.

Now it feels like a secret place, a womb, where I can abandon myself, dive into my feelings with no fear or pressure from the world outside, as if it miraculously dissolved.

Empty and silent, the studio is pulling me into its vortex of creation. Feverishly, I cover the walls from top to bottom with very large sheets of paper. I am getting ready to indulge in creation, to dive body and soul into its core, ready to answer the call of the mysterious unknown. I am going to paint the whole space around myself, to fill every inch of it with color and form.

I start to work on the right side and move toward the left, using ladder and stools, watching the images and colors reveal themselves under my passionate brush strokes. I have no plan. The miracle of spontaneity slips into the room and takes hold of me, guiding me. Exotic plants, multicolored birds, people of all colors, spirits are born, dancing with light and rhythm. My hand moves on its own. I watch with delight the fulfillment of my dream.

I paint for many days from morning till night, all by myself, inside my own painting. I arrive just after dawn. It is always dark when I leave. I walk three blocks to the Metro station, amazed at the world outside, mesmerized by Paris and its crowds of tired workers going back home. The activity, the noise, the expressions on the faces fascinate me as the train carries me away, back to Charenton sur Seine, my home, where my young son is waiting for me. I know I won't have strength left or the desire to eat. I will just take my baby to bed with me and we will cuddle. I will wrap my arms around him, his feet touching my folded knees, and our breath will mix. He will feel completely enveloped by me, relax, and then gently fall asleep.

Now it is time to put the last stroke on the painting. I let myself slide all the way in it. I feel its full embrace. I stand in the most intimate fashion, in the closest way possible, at the center of my own passion. I am ecstatic. God's beauty fills me; my soul is full. Hidden in Paris, in a former meat freezer, I feel the greatest, the fullest lover's embrace.

That night, as I walk out of the studio, my soul is drunk. I am transparent. The whole world could pass through me without touching me. Only an old instinct guides me home.

The next morning, pulled like a magnet, I have to go back. I slowly and carefully open the door to the studio, holding my breath. The world of my painting is still standing in a vortex of energy. Joy and gratefulness burst in me. I softly walk to the center of the room, and suddenly I hear its heartbeat . . . the heartbeat of creation . . .

I stay there and listen. I do not know how much time has elapsed. But at a certain point, I wake back to the world and know that the next step is to take down the painting this very day and free the studio for the next painters.

Slowly, with great respect, I disassemble the immense painting and stack the sheets. The painting disappears, one piece at a time, eaten by the powerful force of the void. Creation breathes in and out, comes and goes.

Nobody has seen my painting. I never looked at it again. Done for its own glory, its gift is still in me. Creation does not need anything added to it, no reward, no approval, no praise. Creation is a moment filled with spirit, a moment when the soul reaches far and brings back God's heart. Done for its own sake, it is free.

Life is movement; creation only a response. The pulse of existence goes on. In and out. No resistance. Creativity fills the moment. In and out. It is as sacred to take my work down as it is to let it unfold. In and out.

4
THE DRAGON
OF CONTROL

Process
Not Control

*If one
Is afraid of losing anything
They have forgotten God's promise.*

HAFIZ

*I*n creativity, there are no standard paths. Points of comparison do not exist. Each of us is so totally unique that our processes are bound to be like no other when we let go of our expectations and travel in our Creative Quest. When you move with process, it is not the object of the hunt that counts, the projected result, it is the journey. It is not where you arrive; it is how you travel.

Your attempts to control the outcome and the evolution of your work can have many levels and escape your attention, especially when feelings are confused with thinking and when preferences take over. Watch for the Dragon of Control, which hides in the smallest places and constantly challenges you to choose between your spontaneity and an enticing result. Can you let go of organizing and planning how your painting will evolve and let it happen naturally step by step? Can you face the Dragon of Control by letting your intuition paint even when entering unfamiliar places and mysterious images?

In creativity, only the process matters—not as a trophy to add to your mantelpiece, but as an exercise of strength and clarity, as an opening to insights and revelations. Linear progress can be planned when you have a goal, when you have a map, but not when you explore the unimaginable unknown. The dreamworld of creation can make your reasonable mind dizzy with its changing grounds. Nothing takes root in it. Nothing can control your intuition; this is its beauty and power. Life flows throughout it, ungraspable, unmeasurable.

Either your intuition or your mind is in control.

If something bothers you don't look at it!

Spontaneous
Expression

I had just started painting with the children a couple of weeks before, when, for no apparent reason, a heavy discomfort grew inside me. I wondered what to do about it but decided not to stop painting. (See paintings nos. 5 and 6.) A wave of sadness washed over me until suddenly I burst into tears. I had not the slightest idea why. At the very same moment, I felt an urge to paint a big truck rolling over my body. With tears clouding my eyes, I dipped my brush in army green and started to paint it. Something moved and guided me from inside—a very new, strange, and lively sensation.

Painting that image was a very dark and drastic thing to do. I felt the thrill of taking a risk and entering the unknown. I knew I was crossing a line. The world out there, I was sure, wouldn't approve. I hesitated for a moment. If I couldn't be myself, what was the point of painting?

In that instant, something clicked inside me that was going to change my life forever. I suddenly became aware of the physical presence of my feelings stored in my chest and stomach. I couldn't have described them, but nothing could have been more real. They stirred in me, and I knew the amazement of having opened a secret door to my own self. I had just touched the immense potential for spontaneous expression in painting.

I proceeded to paint the scene with the truck. Dark feelings spread in me, bringing more tears to my eyes. I painted blood running out of my body. And again, I thought I might have gone too far, that I was out of control! That what I was doing was taboo! The fears of superstition worried me. But there was no turning back from the forces of spontaneous expression.

When I was almost done, I felt the urge to paint the face of the truck driver, but I couldn't. Something inside me signaled me not to. I didn't force it. But as soon as I finished that painting, the next one practically jumped onto the fresh sheet of paper: The driver of the truck had to be painted, and big! Suddenly, I recognized him. Whoa! It was my father! Instantly, anger welled up in me. Despite my mind screaming for me to stop, I threw a few arrows at his image. I worried that I had become a bad and unloving daughter. I had entered the dreamworld where feelings had to express themselves any way they could without being censored or taken literally. Like a child in the sandbox, I could let my spontaneity dictate my play without trying to control the consequences. I could already sense the soothing and healing effect of painting.

I experienced an exaltation I had never known before: the joy of pure and direct expression. For the first time in my life, my feelings and I were moving together. Every feeling expressed created room for the next one to come in. I had found a tool to explore my life, a tool to create space inside my crowded little self where so many feelings were entangled with one another. I had been so lost about what to do with them; now spontaneous expression could guide me. Unexpectedly, I had started my Creative Quest. An immense feeling of gratefulness filled me. I felt truly happy.

Follow
Your Feelings

Each heart beats to a different rhythm
Sounds a different note.

RUMI

Sometimes the Dragon of Control attacks your sense of self, making you self-conscious enough to censor your intuition. It blindfolds you, forcing you to control the feel of your painting and repress your needs of expression. Fight back! Follow your feelings no matter where they take you. Let them unfold and guide you. There are so many feelings waiting to reveal themselves through the sharp sword of your questions. Let creativity fulfill its purpose. *Only what you do not paint is unsafe,* because it keeps turning inside you, creating havoc, trying to free itself.

☙❧

Natalie, a young woman from New York, had an air of thoughtfulness about her. She had just started exploring the painting process and had painted a red-haired girl with a multicolored body. She spent many hours painting lively toned stripes side by side on the torso. The girl's arms were wide open, and her curved black legs crossed as if in dance. The surrounding space was stark white.

Feel and Paint

"I feel people are watching me," she confided anxiously, in a very low, embarrassed, and somewhat resentful voice. "I feel I have to present myself to all these people," she said, indicating the other painters in the room. "I feel I have to show them who I am through my painting. I am becoming very tense and controlled. I feel pressure to perform."

"It does not matter what you think the causes of your control are. The fact remains, you have lost your freedom. You need to go back to Point Zero. What question would help you regain your freedom?" I asked.

Natalie thought for a moment. "If nobody was watching me, what would I do?"

When she asked the question, I saw a dark shadow pass over her face. I questioned her with my eyes.

"When I let go of control, I felt afraid," she replied, a little shakily.

"How could you give room for what you are feeling?" I asked next.

"What would I paint if I could be as afraid as I am and not censor myself?" she said with surprising courage and clarity. She went in. "I do sense a somber black presence on the right side—more an animal than a person, but some of both."

"Is it doing anything?" I asked.

"It is approaching the girl near her stomach. Oh!" she said, alarmed. "It is biting her!"

With that, Natalie went to work. She grinned the whole time she was painting the fierce black creature with sharp teeth. She was amazed at how her feelings had miraculously moved to a deep level. The man-beast turned out to be much larger than the girl and quite threatening. She didn't fight it; she had surrendered to her intuition because inside she experienced a brand-new feeling and felt the joy of expressing herself.

"I would never have thought of it," she said. "This experience has opened a whole new world for me about what I can do!"

Natalie had met the Dragon of Control and had slashed it with her genuine questions, her own authentic weapons. She felt like a warrior. She had entered the mystery of her inner world; she had cut a new path for herself. Now her dream could unfold.

The Dragon of Control has many faces; don't let it fool you with cleverly disguised arguments.

Let Your Body Sense
Your Questions

*A*sking a question mechanically doesn't work. A question is meant to make you change levels of awareness and response and gets you to relinquish control of your thoughts. It requires that you become present and really listen with your insides. Your body needs to be very attentive because so much is stored in it and nothing escapes it. It might respond through some small sensations like pressure, a hot or cold feeling, a tingling, a light change in heartbeat, a mysterious stirring, or a sense of expansion. These are all good signs that you are on track with yourself. Pay attention. These sensations won't last. They are the waking up, the unblocking of feelings or perceptions that have been static for a long time. They are signs of life moving through us with its healing. The body never lies.

෨෧

Amelia, an enigmatic young woman, had spent the entire morning painting with determination. She had painted a large blue-green egg in the center of her painting and a tanned woman lying underneath it, her red hair floating in the wind. Magenta threads were twirling in and out of the top of the egg.

"I first thought my painting had to do with the joyous expression of the feminine, but when I came back from lunch and looked, it felt more like an Eastern archetype. Now I am not sure anymore and don't know what to do."

"Did you inquire through questions?" I asked her.

"Yes," Amelia said. "I could do a Buddha head, but I don't know where."

"Did you really listen to your questions?" I prodded.

"Yes, I did understand the question," she answered blandly.

"If you don't let yourself feel the questions, then you are in your head, a prisoner of your prejudices, trying to control the answers. You are staying on the surface where habits have taken over. Inwardly nothing is going to move. When you listen to your question, what do you feel in your body?"

"Nothing!" she said. "I feel the question only in my head."

"Well," I said, "let's ask again, and this time listen with your whole being. Do you feel any particular sensations, pressures, heat or cold, weight, tingling, anything unusual? What about your breathing? Your heartbeat? What about the soles of your feet or your hands? Can you enter inside yourself, slide into your body?"

She went in, and her eyes suddenly seemed to wake up. "Now I feel the question here," she said, touching her stomach. "I feel a weight . . . with hard edges and strange feelings inside. It's churning." Then, almost instantly, she added, "I could paint a long green snake under the woman's body."

"Can you check if there is anything else?" I asked, challenging her a little further.

"Lots of little gold snakes are moving in circles inside the sun. But I am afraid I am forcing something. I suddenly feel very uncomfortable," she confided.

"Your body is giving you a sign. Something else is trying to come up. Find out what it is. Why don't you try repeating the question?" I suggested.

She did, and then opened her mouth slightly and left it open for a moment while she stared at her painting. "A man is coming toward the woman," she said, stunned. By her reaction, it was obviously not just any man. "I guess I have to do it," she added and started painting him instantly.

"This is not at all what I had expected," she told me later while painting green stripes on a lively snake wrapped around the man. The question pushed me to another place in me that I was not aware of. It pushed me beyond."

When you allow questions to be felt and bring their own sensations, images appear on their own out of the great mystery of who you are.

Anatomy of
Creative Blocks

If he closes off every passage way
And escape route
It's because he wants to show you
A secret way which no one knows.

RUMI

reative blocks are intelligent manifestations of the creative process trying to reorient you in the direction most suited to your soul. They are the challenges you meet during your Creative Quest; they test you and, in doing so, bring out your creative strength. If you face them with understanding, they stimulate you to come from a deeper place and to use yourself more fully. Nothing can release a creative block except a true movement toward yourself.

Creative blocks are made out of your will, your conditioning, and your beliefs. They are made out of ego-building ideas woven into a thick barrier. They are always caused by your trying to force or control something that does not belong in your painting—an idea, an image, a color, a meaning, or a resolution.

You experience a block when you try to make yourself paint

something that deep inside you really don't want to paint but are totally convinced that it is what you must paint. You insist on thinking you know what is right despite your feelings pulling you elsewhere. When you are in that mode, you are attempting to include in your work shapes and images that belong to your rational mind, not to your dreamworld. Your righteous ideas are intruding into the sacred space of creation. The *should* and the *have to* are leading the way to a deadend.

Creativity asks you to sacrifice your blocks into the fire of intuition. The recipe is simple: You take your creative block and ignite it with your questions. By throwing your blocks into the fire, by allowing them to be consumed, you open the way to the unexpressed and the unknown. You empty yourself of old baggage; you clear space for creative energy to pass through. That inner gesture of surrendering sparks your soul because it is not an ego-oriented action.

Every block is an opportunity to go deeper into your Creative Quest. By looking at creative blocks, you look at yourself; you see your patterns and your lack of authenticity. Every block is a stepping stone, a reminder. As long as any tendency to control remains within you or any fears are in the way of your creative freedom, blocks will appear.

The creative block is both a locked door and a key, depending on how you use it.

Reaching
the Core

*T*o reach Point Zero, you need to retrace your steps home, toward yourself. You need to return to the place before your judgments took over. Every judgment or criticism brings a desire to control your images and colors. To find your freedom, you must identify and lift *all* the judgments that are in your way. To build questions powerful enough to transport you back to Point Zero, you may need to destroy layer after layer of impediments to reach the core.

Your judgments are the fuel that will light your way back to Point Zero, the land of your intuition. Your question is only the match. The quality of the fuel defines the amount of heat released. You must be willing to admit to yourself your criticisms, stubbornness, or fears; discovering them is gathering wood for your creative fire.

When you can't find an answer to a question, it is a sign that you are holding on to deeper layers of judgment. Probably something closer to the core. Search for it.

⚬

Paul, a tall lively man in his early forties, came to the workshop. He had not painted since kindergarten. By the second day, he shared with the group that although he does not believe in life in outer space, he had found himself painting a starship with an alien coming out of it. "It has been a thrill and quite unexpected," he said. "I am looking forward to what happens next."

The following session Paul called me over, and said, "I don't know what to do next. I am afraid I am painting with too much precision, too carefully. I feel stuck. I think I might need to do big strokes but there is not enough room."

"What about going back to Point Zero?" I suggested.

"What would I paint if I could do anything?" he asked himself.

"No! You need first to undo the judgment that closed the door to your inspiration. *When intuition stops moving, there is always a controlling thought behind it,*" I said.

"Okay," he said. "What if I didn't have to be so precise and so perfect and control everything, what would I paint next?"

Nothing moved in him.

"It is important to find the root judgment, the one that closed the door to your inspiration. There must be another judgment that holds your creative door shut. What could it be?" I questioned.

"I thought that I should come up with a new, interesting image. Yes, that's the pressure I have put on myself! I thought I should paint another alien, but I really don't feel like it."

"You can undo that attempt to control by another question," I suggested.

"What would I do if I didn't have to find another strikingly interesting image?" he grinned. A slight inner movement had happened but not enough to go on.

"There has to be another judgment underneath the other two, probably something nearer to your heart. Can you let yourself feel it? You see, the questions are bringing you closer and closer to the root blockage. When you get to the core, you'll know it instantly. It is important not to give up. You are learning to reach inside yourself and to free your creativity power."

"When I was asking the last question, I felt insecure and lost. I became disturbed."

"Maybe you are making the assumption that you should not feel stirred up and insecure when you are on the Creative Quest. Could you start your new question from there and find out if it is the root cause?" I suggested.

"What would I paint if it was really okay for me to not be in control and to feel insecure and nervous?" he asked. "Yes!" he said, instantly energized. "Yes! I could paint insects! I could paint big dark insects crawling around the alien ship!" he repeated, half-disgusted, half-excited. And suddenly, full of youthfulness and excitement, he exclaimed, "Yeah! I am going to do it!"

Paul had pulled out the threads that hold his judgments together one by one and won the fight against his creativity. "And now, the alien adventure goes on!" he announced joyfully.

Questions aim at stimulating a state of being,
a way of sensing and feeling that is a fertile ground
to artistic inspiration.

Drink and Eat
Your Question

To meet your intuition fully, to let go of the control of your mind, it is not enough to formulate your questions well. You need to listen to them and consume them. You need to let your questions enter your heart and your gut so that you can absorb them and let them work inside you. If you ask questions with only your mind, your answers stay on the surface as concepts. These answers keep you on an intellectual level, allowing the Dragon of Control to keep its grip on you. Creation requires your presence. Listen to your questions carefully. They will bring you back to *where you are* and give you permission to be, to feel, and to express. A well-listened-to question transports you back to Point Zero, to the land of your heart and soul. There, your intuition flows effortlessly and takes on the subtle images and colors of your dreamworld.

❧

Carole, a pretty young woman with a petulant smile, had a passion for creativity. She had painted herself with a long, flesh-toned body and a deep blue man beside her. The woman had a dark hole in the middle of her stomach.

Carole had been idle for a few minutes when she called me over. "I don't know what to do next," she said, her eyes filling with tears of frustration.

"You obviously have a lot of feelings," I said. "Why don't you let your intuition guide you?"

She nodded. "I used to paint a lot, about every week, but I have not done so in a long time. I feel very scattered and disturbed." Her face became grave. "And my grandfather died last week. I was very close to him." There was a painful silence.

"What questions could you ask to find what you need to paint next?" I asked her.

"If I could paint anything, what would I do?" she asked herself, then answered, "I would paint boredom."

"Oh, no! That is a concept," I told her.

"I would paint anger, then," she attempted, with a little more feeling in her voice.

I shook my head. "Anger is another concept. Staying at that level is a way to stay in control. *True intuition speaks with images, not words.* Ask yourself that question one more time," I suggested.

"If I could paint anything, what would I do?" she repeated.

"Try to be more precise with your question," I told her. "You need to build your question out of what stops you. Judgments and fear of feeling may be blocking you. Your question should be oriented to release feelings by addressing your judgment about them directly and giving yourself permission to feel what you are feeling. Then, images will arise in your consciousness. But you need to really hear your question. You need to feel your question, to drink it and eat it with your whole being."

Carole tried again with a different question. "What would I paint if I could have my feelings go all over the place and be as scattered as I want?" Suddenly, she let out cheerful laughter that wouldn't end.

"Good!" I said. "You have let yourself hear the question this time. Now, let your intuition answer. Intuition is always there waiting for a chance to express itself. Listen to it; it might not be in the way you expect."

"I want to paint my father on the left side of the painting," she exclaimed.

"Can you sense him?" I asked.

"Yes," she said. "He has a beard; he is frowning."

I looked at her; she still seemed half-present. "Are you sure you are letting yourself feel all you can? To check if some feelings are still hiding, you need to repeat the question or ask a new one. When intuition is fully active, there is a particular sense of relief and expansion because you let go of control. Would you like to try one more time?" I suggested.

She did: "What would I paint if I could let myself feel disturbed?" she inquired. "Oh! I see my grandfather smiling on the right," she responded, moved to tears.

Carole painted her father with red strands coming out of his chest and going into hers, wrapping around her heart.

A little later, she spotted me from the corner of her eye and, turning to me, said, "My grandfather is up there on the right corner, in soft blue. I want to paint him next." Then she gazed out the window into the big Taos sky, a warm longing enveloping her.

A well-listened-to question pulls the painter away from tracks of thinking. Attention, then, can rest on something much closer to the need of the heart.

Are You
a Shrinker?

hrinkers are people who shrink spontaneous images when they paint them in an effort to control how they appear. They reduce their size to make them more acceptable or nicer or simply not as threatening. In reality, they shrink the feeling. All of us have shrinkers inside. We have a tendency to minimize what we think of as disturbing. The controlling part of us, then, does the shrinking. Usually it happens so fast that we don't have time to realize what we are doing.

Shrinking needs to stop because everything that is shrunk does not have full expression and will stay inside us, turning round and round, waiting for an opening. It will surface again and again until we surrender to its need. Since we do not know we are shrinking images, I recommend we exaggerate the size of an image any time we feel threatened. Let's try to make it bigger than our first impulse, inflate it, or at least question its size and see what kinds of feelings it brings. Catch yourself in the shrinking act!

*What do you feel is the true size of your image—
not the real size—the true inner size?*

Repeat:
A Good Sign

Doing something more than once is often thought of as being uninventive and uninspired. It attracts the Dragon of Control, which loves to struggle with it. There are two kinds of repeats, however—a controlled repeat and a spontaneous repeat. The controlled repeat is done out of frustration when you feel there is nothing else to do. The spontaneous repeat happens when a deep feeling is met and needs to be explored; intuition, then, brings the images back, again and again.

The full expression of certain feelings can happen only through repetitions. Repeats can be aimed at a representative image, a pattern, or even dots. When it happens, you may feel that you could go on repeating the same thing forever. In fact, the repeat of images is apparent only because every spontaneous repeat is unique. All repeats have their characteristics and life spans and differ in more ways than you generally notice at first glance.

Repeats signal substance rather than dullness. You must know that the Dragon of Control challenges only the repeats of those painters who have reached the depths of the forest. Dragons try to discourage painters from going further by making them think they are wasting their time. When challenged and defeated, the dragons open the treasure caves where repeats pile up and turn into pure

gold. During repeats, the painter is actually exploring some new inner ground, some place out of the way, some secret area difficult to reach.

∞

Henrietta, wornout from a high-pressure job, came to painting for recovery and self-expression. A very emotional person, she became discouraged easily. She had an acute need to understand how her process worked and inquired often.

Henrietta had just painted a couple of women in pastel colors on two pieces of paper that stood as tall as she was. She came to talk to me.

"What is wrong with me? Why can't I come up with something new? I have already painted these people a few times! I keep repeating the same thing again and again! I repeat! I repeat! I repeat!" she exclaimed, angry with herself.

"If whenever God made a baby, He said the same thing, humanity would be in big trouble," I offered, with the hint of a smile.

"I believe I am stuck," she insisted, ignoring my comment.

"You have made a decision that repeating is wrong," I told her. "You have limited your freedom to a narrow space so your inspiration has gone. You need to go back to Point Zero and open all possibilities for yourself. You need to let go of control. What kinds of questions could you ask that would allow you to paint what you need, whether you repeat or not?"

"What could I paint if I could paint anything I want?" she asked, but nothing happened in her.

"Why don't you try to address the question directly from where you are now, with your belief and feelings of the moment? You must start where you are, to open the gate you just closed, and give yourself permission," I suggested.

"I got it," she said. "The question is, What would I do if I could repeat and repeat and repeat as much as I want?"

And she hit to the core. Henrietta answered her own question instantly. "I would paint one more of these people again, her arms would be around the other one. I would like to do that!" she said, suddenly relieved and humored.

I smiled at her. "Write that question in gold letters and keep it close to you. It is your question at this point."

To repeat is a good sign. It happens when you have touched within yourself some true depth.

Exploring
Your Dreams

*The dream is the small hidden door in the
deepest and most intimate sanctum of the soul.*
C ARL J UNG

Painting a dream you remember expresses something you already know, putting you in control of the outcome. Dream images are connected to feelings but, however powerful, are from the past. Why not move ahead, dipping directly into your ability to dream? *Why not manufacture a fresh dream while you are awake?*

When you paint intuitively, your creation starts where the dream left off, or the dream and intuitive images are birthed from the same place. The images are conceived by your image-maker, an inner faculty that has the ability to create visually. It is always at work. It constructs from scratch dreams images at night, and during the day it feeds the creator with forms, images, colors, words, movements, and music.

When a dream image stays alive in you, start painting with it, but do not paint the whole dream. Leave a space for the dream to unfold. Rather than paint memories, paint and dream while you are awake and conscious.

Gloria, a nurse who had just relocated to San Francisco from the East Coast, came to her first painting workshop. She was a stout woman with a likable face and a trusting smile.

"I had a dream last night," she shared the second morning of the workshop. "I want to paint it!"

"Would you like to tell me about it?" I asked.

"It's a woman giving birth in a meadow at night," she began. "There are lots of stars in the sky. I could even see the edge of the earth, breathtakingly beautiful. In the dream, I am watching from a distance, and I think the woman needs help. But I am waiting for something. I would like to find out what."

"What is the most vibrant part of your dream? What image resonates most with your feelings at this moment?" I prodded.

"A blue veil is covering the woman, but I can see the baby girl coming out. This holds a lot of feeling for me," she said.

"You can do two things at this point: Paint your dream as you remember it, or take one image that moves you deeply and let the painting unfold spontaneously. But you have to let go of controlling it by wanting to resolve it. If you don't let go, you won't be free and will prevent your intuition from guiding you. You would have an agenda and preferences, and the dream of the moment couldn't unfold," I explained.

Gloria was willing to go with the second alternative. A while later she had painted a blue woman giving birth and a red car coming from the other side of the earth, bending as if it were made out of rubber. An old man was at the wheel. She spent a lot of time painting his long white beard and wrinkled face.

Gloria's body seemed to have softened, and she didn't seem to be aware of her surroundings anymore. She had entered her dream whole! When I announced the end of the session, she was startled and let out a little shout. "Oh, no!" Later, with a touch of amazement in her voice, she told me, "I don't know what it means ultimately, but I feel I touched something important."

When you paint from intuition, you are held in the caring hands of the dream-maker and its wisdom.

Sexuality and Taboos

Painting is a personal affair, an intimate place where you can allow anything to be expressed. Keep in mind that nobody needs to see what you do, so your freedom is protected. You create in your private world. People who control what they paint may not be able to understand or appreciate the beauty of your wild and spontaneous images and their intensity. Sexual images are bound to appear spontaneously. They are too much a part of the makeup of our society and our life. To paint them does not mean that you have sexual problems or that something is wrong with you, whatever your age or situation. These images express the strong energy of sexuality and release an imagery that has accumulated since childhood from movies, advertisements, books, jokes, and fantasies. It is healthy and natural to let yourself paint this so-called forbidden or embarrassing imagery. If a sense of taboo is brought up, let your freedom break it.

☙❧

Bill was a cowboy-artist from the high country, a very likable man with an edge of shyness and a touch of sadness in his eyes. He had just painted a brown horse standing in the middle of the painting with a lovely woman closeby. He had painted quite carefully hun-

dreds of colored lines on the woman's body, making her whole anatomy vague and even blurry.

"I think I am done. I can't think of anything else," he said.

"How could you check if you are indeed finished?" I asked, probing.

"What would I do if I was not afraid to take a risk and overfinish my painting?" he asked himself. He thought a moment and said, half-daringly, "I would paint two pink breasts on the woman."

"Try another question," I suggested. "Find where inside you are in control and build your question on that."

"Well, what would I paint if I could cross the lines of good behavior and not be afraid to be embarrassed in front of all the women in the workshop?" he said, with a nod of his head toward a couple of women painting nearby. He lowered his voice and said, "I would paint a vagina on the woman's body."

"Can you try a step further? You are doing so well already. Let's use that opening," I suggested.

"Oh, no," he said. "More! Are you kidding?"

"You have no idea what could still be there in that secret dreamworld of yours. You must check for what had no chance to express itself yet! What is there to lose? Take it in a fun way; play and dare like a child. Let the wild part of you express itself. There is no limit to possibilities," I told him.

"Okay," he said. "What would I paint if I could allow just about anything at all? Oh!" he exclaimed with a lively spark in his eyes. "I could paint a long erected penis on the horse. The penis could be almost white and turn around and direct itself toward the woman." After a moment of embarrassed silence, he added, "Sure I can do that, as a matter of fact, I would like to do it and the breasts too, and . . . I will just have to keep that painting away from my mother," he said with a humorous smile.

As Bill painted, his whole demeanor changed. He suddenly seemed to inhabit his body more fully. I would have sworn he had gained a couple of inches in height by the time he was finished. Bill had just reclaimed what belonged to him: the right to his dream-world.

Permission
to Be Bad

A carpenter doesn't scrape a stick to hurt it
He has something in mind for it.

eing "bad" means crossing the lines of the so-called acceptable. It's moving beyond prejudice, your own or others. "Being bad" is actually freeing yourself from a narrow code of
behavior and giving yourself permission to be spontaneous! Break
the boundaries that enclose you. You are on your Creative Quest,
and fences need to be taken down, gates opened.

Beyond them, there are always dormant but intense feelings.
This level of feeling is guarded by the Dragon of Control. *The
Dragon of Control does not want you to take risks.* It is attempting to
turn you away from your path of exploration and tries to keep you
within well-accepted boundaries. The lack of inspiration is a cover-
up; actually, you are full of feelings dying to express themselves.
But they are not what you expect them to be and may shock you.
The feelings that need to be felt are outside your familiar way of
sensing yourself.

The size of the Dragon of Control can be overwhelming if you

take it too seriously. The fear of crossing lines of behavior brings an opportunity to test your strength by fighting for what you really feel and need.

∽

Joan, an independent gray-haired woman, was determined to go to the bottom of her dreamworld and pull from it all the images she could without shrinking. She had painted a reddish man-creature with a long triangular face. Its black spine protruded from its back like a row of spikes. On the upper right of the painting, a black creature-like face had later appeared, opening its shrieking mouth filled with batlike teeth.

When Joan came back the next morning, she said, "I am really stuck. Last night I went home after painting that black face and felt exhausted and blah. This morning, I tried and tried to get some energy started in me, but without the slightest success. Nothing came. I am completely blocked everywhere, every part of me, every place, every level! Everything has stopped. There are no possibilities left!"

"What kind of question could stir back some enthusiasm and inspiration in you? What could bring you back to Point Zero?" I asked.

"I already asked myself questions, and I got the black face in the corner. I did it, and it didn't do anything for me. Nothing moved during or after!" she complained.

"Try to overcome the Dragon of Control. It is attempting to steer you away from your deepest feelings. What other question could you find now to go back to Point Zero?"

"I can't find any other question," Joan said stubbornly. "I already tried!"

"Start where you are," I told her. "You are obviously discouraged. Can you let yourself feel it, be there in the middle of that frustration and ask a question from that place, a question giving you permission to feel what you are feeling and *especially* what you are not expecting to feel?"

"If I could let myself be disturbed, what would I do?" Joan said aloud. Nothing moved. "If I could have anything happen on my painting, what would I do?" Still, nothing moved.

"Try to open the protected place in you, the holding place, the part of you that hides and contracts," I urged. "Start there. Use your frustration as a building block of the question. You do not have to behave. *You do not have to keep control of everything you paint!* You do not have to be good!"

"Oh!" she said, suddenly stimulated. "What would I paint if I could be . . . bad . . . bad! I would paint . . . Yes! A big penis on him," she said, pointing to the reddish man-creature."

"How big?" I asked to challenge her a little further.

"Very big!" she answered shamelessly, pointing across the length of the painting.

I came back later; Joan had in fact painted a very long, beige penis and decorated it with purple netlike designs and red strands coming from its base. She looked relaxed, even radiant.

"You had quite a shift of energy," I commented.

"This is not a penis," she told me. "What I painted is penis energy! The question giving me permission to be bad really got me going!" she added with a smile of satisfaction. "It did it for me!"

*By daring to paint so-called unacceptable images
or colors, you build your creative power.*

The Power of
Embarrassment

Futile the winds
To a heart in port.
EMILY DICKINSON

When you create, embarrassment is always a good sign. It means that you have crossed the line of the familiar zone. You have left the no-risk area for a truly alive ground. You have moved into a new territory and have entered the land of exploration, the wilderness of your soul. You are now facing the Dragon of Control and have stopped running away anytime something challenges you or does not fit your expectations. If you feel embarrassed, let yourself be intrigued. Don't censor or control your natural inclinations. You are on your way to discovery. You are exploring the wilderness of your Creative Quest.

An earthy and wild young woman, Ginnie had stood all her life for what she believed. She loved to play and to go to the edge of her freedom. My workshop gave her an opportunity to do this. Her painting portrayed a couple of women, one red, one purple. The purple one was pressing her hand on the other one's chest.

Ginnie called me over to her and said, "I could paint a bruise on the chest, but I am not sure it is what I really want to do. I was feeling confident before; I feel uncomfortable and hesitant now."

"How could you find out what you really want to paint?" I asked her.

"By doing it I suppose and seeing how it makes me feel," she answered.

"Is there a shorter route?" I asked. "What questions could you ask yourself?"

She went inside. "What else could I paint on the chest if I didn't do bruises?" she asked aloud.

"Oh, no! That question would make you search for an idea around the chest, tying you there. It is too directive; you need to go back to Point Zero, inside yourself, where anything is possible *anywhere*, so that what you need will have a chance to appear."

Ginnie went back inside, determined to find a question that worked. "What would I do if I was not afraid to be inconsistent or even ruin my painting?" She slowly repeated that question three times, as if to absorb it deeply into her bones.

I saw her flush suddenly, but she remained silent.

"What was the answer?" I asked.

Looking into my eyes, visibly embarrassed, she mumbled, "A man, fully aroused, is coming straight up from the bottom of the painting."

"What color?" I asked

"Flesh color, yes, it is there . . . and . . . oh . . . there is another one here," she added as she pointed to the space between the women's bodies.

Ginnie, a courageous spirit, went for it. A few minutes later, she said, "This is exactly what I needed. I felt very exposed first. I wanted to run away and hide, but it really felt right. I would never have thought about it! That question brought it out."

I watched Ginnie paint for a few minutes. She shone with the inspired look of those who dare to trust their intuition and stand for who they are.

Any attempts, no matter how subtle, to control the outcome prevent the true expression of who you are.

Suspicion of
Spontaneity

When I asked a group of my students if they were suspicious of their spontaneity, ninety-nine percent of them said they were. They reluctantly admitted that whenever they felt a spontaneous urge, their response was guarded. They were watching out just in case spontaneity would take them to an unwanted or threatening place.

"I couldn't systematically and under every circumstance trust it!" said one of the painters.

You trust your spontaneity or you don't. If you are suspicious, it is because you treat spontaneity like an outside force, like a stranger in your home. You keep a constant eye on it, lest it does some damage or steals from you. In fact, spontaneity lives in you and flows in your blood. It is part of your being as surely as is your arm or leg.

Are you suspicious because you cannot control spontaneity, because it might not follow your desires and expectations? Did you forget that spontaneity's main purpose is to get you to jump out of your mapped tracks? It carries what you need, whether it be consciously wanted or unwanted. Wisdom moves your intuition; it knows you and knows what you need. Spontaneity won't misdirect you, for it is both in you and of you. If you think you have to control and censor such an integral part of yourself, if you are suspicious of your spontaneity, you won't travel far on your Creative Quest.

෧෨

Many years ago, I had painted a large blue Buddha sitting cross-legged and on each side of him a big tree. The trees were the trees of dissolution, where people in the process of giving up self-centeredness go to finish drying up their thinking minds. Gray and green heads with hollow eyes were hanging from each bare branch. I felt the spontaneous urge to hang my own head with the others, but I feared I might dissolve myself if I kept painting. Discomfort loomed in; resistance mounted. I felt weak. An hour went by. I came to a point when I could hear myself saying that I could not take anymore and that wherever I had gone was far enough. I stopped listening to my intuition.

My spontaneity did not put up a fight. It simply withdrew to a more superficial level. I had missed an opportunity. I did not realize what I had done because I assumed I would return soon to that vibrant point of exploration. I never did, at least not in the same way. In fact, it took a long time to even come close to that place again. To this day, I wonder what would have happened if I had not interfered.

Never again did I say no to my intuition. I understood that *what is given is always within the realm of the most desirable* and never, ever, too much to take. Spontaneous expression takes us to bridges we need to cross—a point of passage where the known ends and the unknown starts. Intuition asks us to cross, no matter what. It is not concerned whether we walk or leap or swim or dig a tunnel. It wants us to reach the other side. Circumstances design the means.

When suspicion ends, the creative process is freed from the struggle of choice, from the need to take a detour, to watch, to guard, to protect. The safety of creation envelops us. The fact is, nothing is too terrible to see or feel once we trust. For, just beyond that edge where spontaneity takes us, we feel at home. There, no stranger exists, nor ever could exist—only the moment with its fullness of being.

5
THE DRAGON
OF MEANING

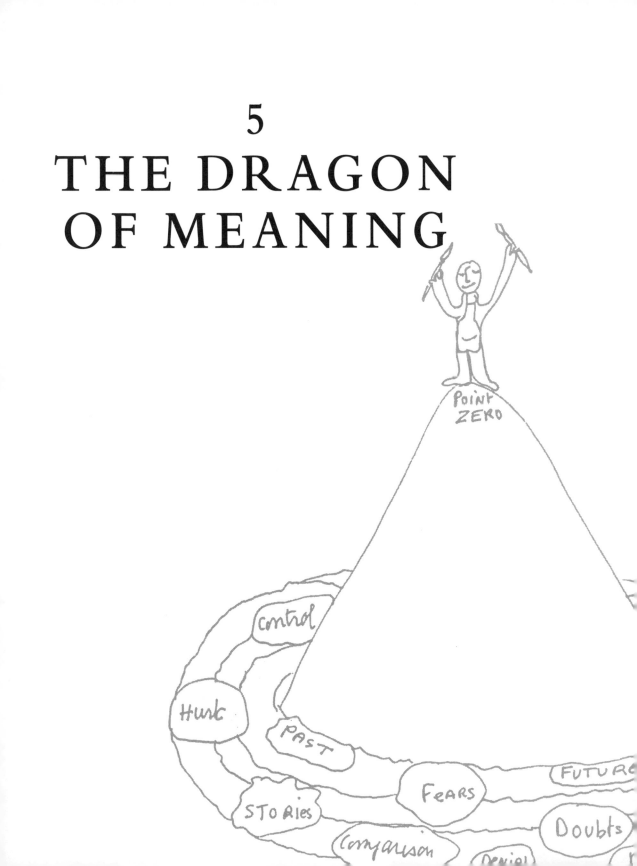

Caught Up in
a Story

Exploration separates us from astonishment,
which is the only gateway to the incomprehensible.
Eugene Ionesco

While painting, images are often processed by the mind, explained and categorized. The Dragon of Meaning blows its fire of reason and literal explanation to everything in view. It thrives on chaining painters to their thoughts. Like a spider's web, painters wrap stories around themselves until they can't move. Prisoners of their own making, they often don't escape the force of their own suggestions. The momentary pleasure of a storyline is the powerful bait. But the story, churning in the artist's head, signals the end of adventure, the end of genuine exploration. The painter then follows only one track, the story's track. The truly alive, the unexpected, has no room to move in. Discovering how to shift your source of inspiration through questions is then necessary to break free of the sticky web and overcome the dragon's spell.

೧೨

Amy, an unusually enthusiastic and passionate woman, just painted a double-sized painting, a large, white net filled with people stacked

on top of one another. A huge, open red mouth was pulling the whole net into itself.

"I am stuck in the meaning," she volunteered. "I can't stop thinking about the story I created around these images. I lost my freedom. I feel paralyzed!"

Amy was afraid to make the wrong move, to lose the thread of an interesting plot. There was no room for spontaneity or adventure in her painting.

"What questions could you ask yourself to regain your freedom?" I asked her.

She thought for a moment, then asked herself, "What could come out of the mouth?"

"Oh, no! Not that question," I replied. "That would further the story. It is too directed. It would take you right into a psychological loop or even a swamp! You need to come back to Point Zero, *a place before stories are born.*"

Amy hesitated and then asked herself with a lukewarm voice, "What would I do if I was free?" She stared at her painting for a moment and coerced an image out of herself. "I would paint a snaky purple thing here!" she said, somewhat discouraged, pointing at the dark bottom of the painting.

"No," I say again, "you do not need to look for an image. You need to jump out of your mental tracks and go back to feeling. You can do that by using your block and opening it up by giving yourself permission. You need to include the block in the question. What question could you create?"

She looked right into me and asked with gusto, "If I didn't have to wonder what it all means and where I need to go, what would I paint?" Suddenly, a shift happened; her face moved from the inside. "I feel terrified!" she burst out.

"Good! Stay there; the next step, the next image will come on its own," I suggested, relieved that she had finally let herself feel.

When I came back a few minutes later, Amy had painted big white cracks in the large net.

"It makes me feel expanded," she said.

"What happened in you that allowed you to paint the big cracks?" I inquired.

"I let go of the story," she answered.

"Oh, then, could we say that the problem was trying to control the meaning of your painting?" I asked with a smile.

Amy smiled back. Her face took on a shade of wisdom as she looked right into my eyes and nodded.

The source of your images comes from beyond your mind, from a place before knowing.

Seduction
of Content

The content of your creation and its meaning offers what you think you want most, something you can identify with: your stories and their messages. The mind is tempted to fill its pockets with symbols and interpretations. It often gathers them until you become so heavy that you can no longer create.

In truth, the unsecured ego uses the content of the painting to feed itself, to gorge itself fat. True creativity does not rehash stories or look for resolutions. It wants you to move into the unknown and explore. Creativity invites you to practice emptying your stories and letting go of the known meaning. Your mind can only come up with what it knows; all it can do is rearrange and reorganize what is already there. On the other hand, creativity works at undoing assumptions. You need to break from what you think you are, from your homemade life story. Your intuition allows your world to ex-

meaning

pand far beyond the warehouse of your mental pictures. It can take you as far as you allow it, assuredly farther than any personal story.

By identifying with content, you become trapped. This can happen easily because the seduction of content has many strategies. They could be, for example, "If I use only light colors, I will eliminate the darkness in my life," or "If I paint my mom fighting with my dad, I will resolve my childhood issues," or even, "If I paint death, I will diminish my fear and vulnerability." The basic consequence of these strategies locks you inside the problem or issue you are trying to work on. It stops the natural flow of creation by closing the door to the unexpected because it defines who you think you are as a static entity.

ဆာ

Burt, a man in his fifties, gentle and well behaved, was bored. He had painted a picture of himself and his girlfriend. In it, he was pushing her away. He had tried to make her scream by painting her mouth wide open. He had circled her eyes with red to show anger. To darken the scene, he had painted black shadowy forms behind his figures. This symbolic scene could have been quite intense, yet strangely, no spark animated the painter or the painting.

"I really don't know what to do next. I don't feel inspired," Burt said. The temptation of content had seized Burt. The story had taken over.

"Burt, what question could you ask yourself to find out if you are interested in what you are doing, and, if not, what it is that you would rather paint?" I asked.

"What could I paint if I didn't have to paint my relationship, right now?" he asked. "What I really like to do is paint the heavens," he answered quickly, with a touch of nostalgia. "But I thought

I should paint my relationship because we have been having problems recently," he added grimly.

"Burt, did you think you could help your problems by painting what you know about them? It does not work that way. Painting a story only confirms what you already know! What you need is to go to Point Zero and discover what you do not sense and cannot imagine. This will bring healing."

Freed from the idea of what he had to do, Burt started a new painting—blue-lavender heavens with angelic beings floating amidst soft clouds. He became totally absorbed in it. Suddenly, a woman face's appeared, smiling, among the clouds.

He turned to me with an astonished look on his face. "I'm painting my mother!" he said, touched to the heart. "It has been such a long time since she died!"

*Being seduced by content and meaning
makes you a slave to your thoughts.*

Fighting with the Universe

Don't be a fool!
Nothing can grow until
the ground is turned over and crumbled.

RUMI

The inner world of your thoughts and feelings is the world of your dreams, with its image-maker and its wisdom. Let yourself wander in your dreamland! Don't try to reshape your inspiration into something familiar. The parts you don't recognize and the parts you don't understand are the most powerful parts of your dreamworld because these parts have escaped your judgment and control. Congratulate yourself for having gone beyond the expected. No need to fight, manipulate, or smooth things out. Never worry about the meaning of your images. Like in dreams, the intelligence of creation guides you toward harmony and expansion. Surrender, let creation happen; you are in the hands of the universe.

Jennie came to the workshop in the midst of family difficulties. She cried most of the day, judging herself for her past behavior with her son, questioning the state of her heart and the depths of her motherly feelings.

She called me over. "I am stuck," she said. "I have painted one image after another as they came to me, yet I feel nothing. Nothing has happened; nothing has moved," she explained, defeated. She had painted a white sailboat and steep mountains in the upper right of the painting, and a valley with a little yellow house in the bottom.

"What about asking yourself questions?" I suggested.

"I have already done that. I asked myself what would I do if I was not afraid. I painted some lightning around my little sailboat, but as soon as it was done I felt I lost something. It ruined my painting!"

"Why do you think you ruined it? Are you telling me that you know the meaning of the lightning and that it is bad? How can you know?" I asked.

Her eyes filled with tears of frustration. "It was a beautiful childhood memory before!"

"Can we agree that you do not know the true meaning of that image? It could mean that something is about to reveal itself or is about to wake. It could be a blessing. It could be so many things! Let it be! Let the unknown be painted. Trust. Your consciousness is limited to what you know, and you interpret from that place. Spontaneous creation is given to you to transcend these limitations.

"Always keep in your heart that creation is benevolent. Can you see that the lightning—whatever its meaning is—cannot hurt you? It is passing through you like the rest of your intuition, aiming at healing not hurting. When you refuse to paint it, you are fighting with the creative energy of the universe.

"The universe brings you lightning. You say, 'No! I don't want it; it means bad,' and then you tell me you are stuck and exhausted!

You have pushed away what came to you spontaneously; you have stopped expressing yourself. No wonder you feel blocked.

"Would you rather follow a technique with step one, step two, step three? Do you really want a map and an agenda, or are you craving for wild spaces or unexpected discoveries? You are in the dreamworld of intuitive painting, in a different reality. You are on a Creative Quest and are experiencing its mysterious manifestations."

"It's happening in my life, too," Jennie admitted suddenly. "I fight. I fight all the time with everything." She cried again.

"What if you could let yourself ask a question that would allow you not to fear your images and do more rather than less?" I asked.

"I can try," she said without a trace of enthusiasm. "What would I paint next if it was okay to have lightning on my painting?"

She got a strange look on her face and went back to painting without uttering a word. I saw her struggling for a little while, then, surprise, a shift happened. Fierce lightning struck her boat from all sides and wild waves crashed into it. Then, all of a sudden, the house took fire.

Had Jennie moved back to the dreamworld of creation, had she entered true play? When I came close to her, she didn't even turn her head to look at me. She kept painting, moved by the great winds of her mysterious dreams.

Your true work, the unfolding of your happiness,
happens as you paint. Understanding comes last.

1

I enter with delight into pure process. I give up progress, product, and goals.

2

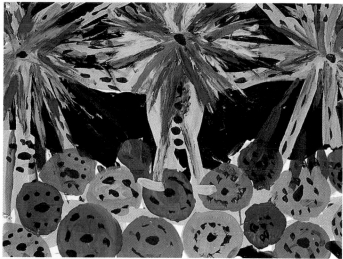

MICHELLE MC

3

Old feelings resurface. Intensity builds.
I enter the secret garden of my life.

7

9

*My brush spontaneously finds new
ways to paint. Colors blur and
then melt into one another,
expanding my skill.*

10

There is no other purpose than
to paint freely and explore.
I watch amazed as images
appear without choice.

11

12

13

Images form in me like dreams. Each one, its own universe.

14

15

16

My hand follows
the inner call.
I tiptoe, I run,
I embrace, entranced.

Spontaneous creation pulls
me into the vast mystery
of existence.

The intimacy of painting allows me to explore wild and spontaneous images.

18

19

20

21

22

Energy rushes through my body like a torrent.
The strangest visions visit me.

23

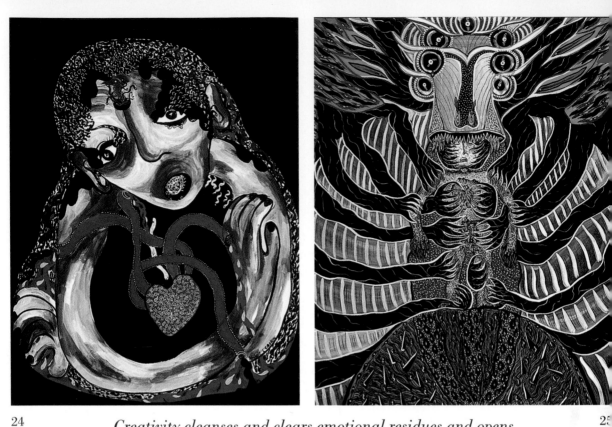

24

Creativity cleanses and clears emotional residues and opens passageways for blocked energy.

Intuition pulls me into the mystery of life and death. New perceptions infiltrate my familiar world, transforming it.

*I paint those waiting
in line to be born.
The depth of the
miracle of birth
envelops my spirit.*

29

30

31

32

Creation guides me in my
search for the great unknown
all the way to the door
of my longing.

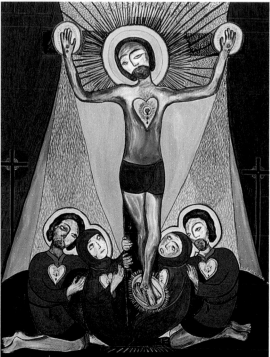

33

*It was moments of
pure joy and
harmony between
my painting,
my experience,
and my self.*

*I wonder about living
on the edge of the
earth, facing the
emptiness, falling
into the stars, melting
down into God.
Who am I?*

Going the Whole Way

When you feel you have already done all you know or can think about, you have a special opportunity. You can challenge the unknown to move in by facing the Dragon of Meaning. You have come to a place where you can access the mystery of expanded perceptions and healing. Creative passion is born out of using yourself fully, all the way to the edge. To explore from that place, you must let go of meaning and dive into the current of a larger creative energy. Go back to Point Zero, listen and look, new dimensions of experience await you.

⚬⚬

Judith was a professional artist with an impressive portfolio. A small woman in her forties with curly gray hair adorning her face in the most charming way, she had come to the workshop to rekindle her passion for painting.

The first day met her with enormous resistance. Judith raged and cried when faced with trying to let go of her habits and patterns. But Judith was not the type to give up; she was going to finish the five-day workshop no matter how hard it might be. She painted semi-abstract images at great speed, producing an impressive amount of paintings. When she got tired of it, she came to me.

"I really want to break patterns," she said. "This is why I am here. What should I do?"

"What question could you ask yourself to stimulate your intuition? What would give you more permission?" I asked.

A curious light sparkled in her eyes. "If I was not afraid to paint something really challenging, what would I do?" she asked herself in one breath. Then, without a pause, she exclaimed, "I know exactly what I would do! I would paint a big body, my own, as a matter of fact, life-size!"

She traced the outline with her finger first, to practice breaking her pattern of painting abstractions instead of real images. Then she dipped her brush in the beige paint and started; it was delicious

to watch the ease and joy she experienced, painting her own body, larger than life. When she was finished, she asked, "Now, what else? I want to go all the way! Push me, please, push me!"

"What question would bring out more of you?" I asked.

Intrigued, she said, "What would I do if I didn't hold back anything at all?"

There was a short silence. Then, I heard a muffled, wounded "Oh, no! Oh, no!" Bent over, as if she had just been struck by a shadow, Judith moved to the paints and chose a long brush, dipped it in dark purple, and proceeded to paint a large scar on her painted right breast, tears suddenly flowing down her cheeks.

When she was done, I asked her, "What could be the next step?"

"I have said it all!" she answered instantly. "I had a mastectomy three years ago," she added with a painful look.

"The Dragon of Meaning has just caught you, trying to prevent you from exploring further! You have said all you knew," I replied. "What about the other part, the mysterious part of your feelings, of your life? You now have the opportunity to let it in. How could you bring forth the unknown dimension? What question would you ask to go back to Point Zero?"

She didn't believe that more could happen in her. Tired, but willing to give it a try, she asked, "If anything unexpected could appear anywhere, what would I do?" Suddenly, she opened her eyes wide as if something astonishing had appeared in front of her. "A white star would fly out of the scar," she said in wonder, "and . . . streams of stars would flow out from a multitude of places on the whole painting." Following her intuition, Judith painted with renewed energy.

I met her later during the day; we talked under the vast Taos sky. "It was a real breakthrough!" she said gratefully. "I saw the *other* dimensions of what happened to me three years ago."

*Every wound expressed is a doorway
to greater dimensions.*

Artificially Simulated
Emotions

When you create, let yourself wander in the land of your quest where dragons have a chance to meet you, where images can wake ancient or latent feelings, where the unknown and its mystery can enter your consciousness. Each meeting with a dragon is an opportunity to further your creativity because dragons always challenge your patterns. By fighting back the Dragon of Meaning, you deepen your creative response. If not by forcing yourself to paint images with meaning that speak to your familiar consciousness, you bar the entrance to your true quest. You spend the great celebration of creation behind closed doors, hearing only echoes of plays and cheers.

♋

Jane, a serious and spiritual person, came to the workshop eager to find depths in her creative process. "I am stuck," she told me.

"What question could unstick you?" I suggested.

She came up with one quickly. "What am I afraid of?" And her eyes became flooded with tears. "My family is in Russia, so far away from me. I am very afraid for them. Maybe I should paint them wounded."

"Where did you get the idea that you should paint what you are afraid of? Where did that come from?" I inquired. "This would be like using a technique and following an agenda. Think about it. You *already know* that fear; nothing can be new there. This is not a creative exploration. It is up to your intuition to discover what is to be painted."

"I thought I should paint what I am afraid of and what I don't want to paint!" she insisted.

"Not at all. You *never* need look for what you are afraid of, but if it comes spontaneously of course you do not want to push it away. This is very different from having the agenda of painting what frightens you. When you look for what frightens or disturbs you, you are artificially simulating emotions. This is not being intuitive or open, but manipulative. You need to go back to Point Zero, enter your dreamworld, move beyond what you know, and journey through your Creative Quest."

"What if I could paint anything at all?" she asked herself, but inside her nothing moved.

"You need to lift the barrier that is stopping you when you ask your question. And you know what is stopping you? It is the belief that you have to resolve your fear for your family. So, what question could you ask instead?"

"What could appear anywhere on my painting if I didn't have to resolve my fear and worries about my family and if I could do anything at all?" When she heard the question, her body relaxed. "I would paint a wild creature in the left corner!" she said.

"What kind?" I asked immediately, to make sure she wouldn't back up.

"A dark blue one with suspicious yellow eyes," she said, showing me with her fingers an elongated-eye shape. "And an open mouth with a thin tongue sticking out!" she added, surprised by her sudden liveliness.

"What other questions could you ask if you could give yourself even more permission? There is no harm in checking if you have gone to the end of what is possible," I suggested.

"How many creatures could I paint if I could have more than one?" Jane asked herself playfully. "A lot of them! Coming from top and sides, they are male creatures!"

She painted three large colorful heads with long, bright-red tongues covered with yellow dots. Then, all of a sudden, a pinkish, sensuous woman appeared at the center of the painting on a rich-blue background, quite a takeoff from her start. Jane had just learned to move through different levels of reality. She had found the secret passageway leading her beyond the controls of her mind. She had fought back the Dragon of Meaning and won.

Jane's eyes were sparkling, her brush eager, the forced images she had struggled with receded far into the background, giving way to the expression of her whole being. "I feel wonderful with a new sense of freedom. Now, I understand about painting passion," she told me with an excited smile.

I assured her that if, at a later time, the images of her family needed to appear, they would surely find their way onto the paper.

Though it is therapeutic, creative painting is not meant to be used to solve problems; its purpose is to bring liveliness, insights, and revelations into the psyche.

Benevolent
Darkness

Shame, darkness, blaming, self-hatred,
Do I shrink from you
Or can I be open and vulnerable to your teachings.

RUMI

*I*f creativity is benevolent, how come all that darkness comes out in paintings?"

Creativity's purpose is to stir back to life what has fallen asleep, to cleanse and clear emotional residues, and to open passageways for blocked energy. So when the currents of creation sweep through us, they carry whatever lies in their way. The unnecessary is put away, like cleaning a garden in springtime. The weeds are pulled out, the debris swept, the dead trees cut down. The death-rebirth principle is at play.

Inside each of us is a storage of unfinished and repressed feelings accumulated during a lifetime or more. You never need to force yourself to paint your dark images, or you will fall prey to the Dragon of Meaning. These hidden emotional pockets, which hold pain and darkness, are *spontaneously* brought to the surface when creativity is unleashed. Denied feelings have intensity and rawness

The Worm

that need to express themselves boldly and freely, with primitive imagery and strong symbols. Dark and light are at work; everything unfinished comes out when the time is right. All is put in motion for healing, harmony, and growth.

As in dreams, the image-maker uses all sorts of imagery to awaken consciousness. It is never afraid of the so-called dark images and even uses them to express the intensity of the light itself.

The creative light, with its powerful force, often needs to disguise itself in its opposite so that we can accept it and get used to it. The dark holds the surgical knife that frees the light. It prepares you for the journey where perceptions change. The train that travels into the light needs no lightbulb. This is why, when you sometimes dive into that so-called darkness in your painting, you feel happy and loving at the end. On the other hand, when you force light or spiritual symbols into your painting, you may feel tense and restless.

The best route is to let the light and the dark come on their own terms and colors. This magical surrendering can fill you with wonder. If you want to meet the mystery, don't take imagery literally. Stop interpreting apparent darkness as dark and violent images as proof of violence in you. Be a little more humble; admit that you don't really know what it all means. To take the images literally would be going back to your little consciousness where everything is explained and organized, to that small space that you hoped to leave behind when you started painting.

When you paint, unknown dimensions move in. For instance, if you paint a knife, you can't know if it is ultimately cleaning up a dead branch or cracking a seed in you or breaking through the shell of your heart or attacking out of anger. Let duality express itself and don't worry about it. *When you embrace duality, resisting nothing, forcing nothing, you rise above it and reach the sacredness of creation.*

How could you know what the spirit looks like visually? It's a mystery. Let your concepts be destroyed. Let the light and dark pass away. To experience more light, more concepts need to be broken. The breaking of these concepts allows you to travel in your dream-world all the way to the spirit. At these times, God wears a black coat. If you can drop the idea of dark and light in creation, you will be free to go much further than you can possibly imagine. You must stop clinging. The so-called dark images are gifts. Can you see their unfailing benevolence pulling you away from the false in you, dispelling ignorance?

When creating, you tap into energy much beyond yourself. The universal energy blends with your own energy, and you manifest both at once no matter what is painted. Images flow by, often intense or dark-looking because you are in the process of breaking patterns and long-held beliefs. The hammer of creation needs to chisel the wood thoroughly before it is able to sculpt its most sensitive work.

*The dark images keep appearing, because for form
and formless to dance together, the mind must surrender
its prejudices, beliefs, and fears.*

The Alchemy of Creation

Blow by blow, slowly, the cheek of the heart
Gets slapped clean.

Rumi

Broken glass, mostly from beer and wine bottles, often ends up on the shore or in the sea. The sea picks up the pieces, and the water currents toss, turn, and twirl the dangerously sharp pieces, softening them, eroding their edges to the smoothest imaginable contour. In time, the currents reshape the glass, sand it, inhabit it, and transform it. The glass takes on an angel-like color, an opaque white or green or even blue shade. When you put sea glass in your hand, your whole body fills with the softness of the water and the spirit of the sea. The alchemy has happened: The cheap glass has become precious stone. The jewel radiates the mystery of the deep water.

When you paint, your images are like sea glass. Your wounds and past hurts are the freshly broken glass with its dangerous edges; the current of your creativity tosses and turns them into precious stones. When, away from mental explanations and meanings, your intuition births your images, the alchemy of creation transforms them into gems. Their beauty vibrates the truth of your soul no matter their gentle, fierce, or even threatening appearance.

During the Creative Quest, you encounter many obstacles. You need to face not only dragons but also the intensity of the wounds and memories that might be released in the process. Unfinished feelings rise unexpectedly on the road, asking you to feel. You need to face them without getting trapped in their meaning for your Creative Quest to move on. You must surrender to what the current brings and let healing happen. The flowing of feelings opens and widens the passageway of creation and brings insights. *The creative currents actually bump into unfinished emotional materials and will keep doing so until they are felt and let go of.* In that way, the creative process takes care of the whole being, clearing the way for the deep exploration of creation.

ᘖ

Sue had a strong personality. By her late twenties, she had already seen much of the world. Intelligent and quick-witted, she wanted to commit to her creativity. She had just painted, with infinite care, a bright torso, representing herself, blue with a peach outline. When I passed by, she spotted me from the corner of her eye. "I am stuck!" she said, ready to fight to the death whichever dragon was stopping her. "I don't know what to do. I was very interested for a while, but now it completely stopped. I can't come up with anything!"

"What question could you ask to get things started again?" I questioned.

"What would I do if I could stop thinking?" she asked herself. She stared with wide-open eyes at her unyielding painting, but nothing happened.

"You need a question that will take down the barriers you unknowingly set for yourself. Can you unzip your own being, let yourself be vulnerable? What is inside you is there anyway; you might as well let it express itself.

"The Dragon of Meaning is guarding a door that hides something you would rather not see. It does not have to be dramatic, but it's close to your heart. The desire for meaning makes you focus on what you think your painting should represent instead of allowing your deeper feelings to unfold. *Don't look with your mind's eye* to find it because whatever it finds won't be what you really need. What you need is to go back to a place of no preference, back to Point Zero, and see where it leads you. You must not look for an idea. The currents of creativity will bring to your consciousness whatever you need. Your job is to stop protecting yourself!"

Her intense eyes looked right into mine as she made herself ready to be inwardly naked. And she did jump into the unknown: "If I didn't protect myself at all, what would I paint?" she asked aloud, but to herself. And it happened. I could almost hear her heart pounding in her chest. "I sense somebody else in the painting," she said in a broken voice.

"What type of person could it be if you didn't protect your feelings?" I asked.

"If I didn't protect my feelings," she repeated and suddenly exclaimed, "Oh, yes!" Her face contracted into a painful expression. Tears burst out. Somebody from her past had suddenly emerged, a man from her teenage years who had left a scar on her heart. She feverishly painted a dark-green man invading her painting while tears from the old wound washed down her cheeks. Then, she quieted and painted for another couple of hours exquisite yellow and green details, lining and outlining everything.

"It's so good to paint. I feel as if a burden was just lifted from me!" she said later, marveling at the miracle of her old wounds slowly turning into gems.

Imagination
or Intuition

*I*magination is the seeing in one's mind of new combinations of images and ideas. Imagination uses what is stored in the conscious warehouse of experience and rearranges or reorganizes it in inventive ways. It is a thinking process. Intuition, on the other hand, comes directly from the vast ocean of not knowing. It comes up with the unexpected and the nonverbal. It lives beyond the reaches of the mind and carries the voice of feelings and spirit.

The mind thinks it has options. A rich imagination could come up with dozens of possibilities within minutes; intuition, however, knows but one answer at every moment. Intuition and imagination do not mix and are used for different purposes. One cannot survive in the other's habitat.

There are many ways to use your imagination against your feelings. Some ways are very blunt, some very subtle. You could, for instance, change size, appearance, form, or color of your spontaneous images. The mind takes the feeling and puts it into a clever idea to avoid being vulnerable. You fall into the trap of your imagination. You believe that you are feeling because you find your idea interesting. You have been seduced by the inventive power of your imagination.

When painting from intuition, you never choose an image, you just find it, obvious, alive, waiting to be painted. It is born naturally out of the womb of your inner world.

Elise, a blond woman in her early thirties, was ready to start painting but moved with anxiety. "I think I want to paint my mother," she announced.

"How big do you want to make her?" I asked.

"Oh, she is very small. She has always been afraid of everything. I'll put her in the corner, ten inches high," she said.

"Tell me, if you stop translating your thoughts into images, what size does she really feel like? Can you let your intuition decide? Can you ask yourself a question?" I asked her.

Taken aback, Elise went inward. "If I didn't have to paint my mother really small, if she could be any size at all, how big would she really be? Actually, she does feel quite big right now," she admitted, pointing to a space that could fill two sheets of paper. "Yes, about that size." Then, struck by a clever idea, she added, "Maybe I could paint her as a big, green, furry creature."

"Elise, you need to find out if that creature is coming from your imagination or from your intuition," I told her. "What about going back to Point Zero? Can you ask yourself a question using the doubt?"

"What would I paint if my mother didn't have to take a non-human appearance?" she asked. Her feelings were quick to respond. Her face turned slightly pale. "Ah! I would paint my mother life-size, in flesh color," she said softly, tears flooding her eyes, her heart, reclaiming for herself her true feelings.

We are all addicted to imagination in some ways,
addicted to feel in the head rather than in the heart.

Being Connected

have seen painters strive and struggle to be connected to their paintings. "I am not feeling connected!" is a very common complaint. What does it mean to be connected? To be connected is to feel that you and your painting are one; you and your painting are floating down the river of your creativity as one unit. While you are exploring that mysterious river, your state may vary greatly depending on the current, the weather, the land you are crossing, the time of day, and the seasons. It is always different. Sometimes it feels quiet, sometimes emotional, sometimes deep; sometimes it may feel scattered or uncomfortable, and sometimes you may even feel lost. At times, you may be extremely calm, even to the point where you doubt if anything is happening. Other times, you might experience an altered state or spiritual revelation. The difficulties arise when you experience discomfort and uncertainty. *Often, the only thing between you and your painting is your personal identification with your idea of being connected!* It is the Dragon of Meaning luring you to demand meaning in your images that relates to your life.

You cannot be connected by trying to be connected. You are connected only when you stop interfering with your natural intuition no matter what it gives you as an experience. Connection with your painting happens when you get out of the way and let intuition do its work.

Dean, a young artist in his thirties with sharp, awake eyes, had worked many hours on a somewhat abstract painting of orange-lavender hills and purple vegetation.

"I am tired. I want to stop. I have no energy left; no more life to put in this painting," he said, discouraged.

"What do you think is the criticism that is stealing your creative energy and blocking you?" I asked.

"I don't really like parts of my painting," he answered. "Some of it is okay, but compared to the past, I am much less pleased than I have been. I have lost interest," he told me.

"What other judgment do you have about yourself? Give me the most pitiless judgment you may have."

"I don't feel connected to my painting," he admitted, obviously upset. *Bingo,* I thought, *here it is, the root cause.* "Could you build a question with that judgment?" I asked.

"What would I paint if it didn't matter if I was connected or not?" he attempted.

"You must feel that question; you must give yourself permission not to strive to be connected."

"I would paint a face screaming in the clouds!" he exclaimed. A half-hour later, Dean had carefully painted a sunset-colored face with a wide-open red mouth. "And these are all the people falling out of the scream," he said, showing me a rain of multicolored little people tumbling from the gigantic scream. Truly there were no more questions about being connected.

Your painting does not have to *look good and* does not have to *make sense.*

Painting from
Your Heart

When you paint from intuition, your heart is being used. Creation passes through it like a mountain river in the spring, melting ice, washing out debris, opening new passageways, clearing up the most precious place of your being. To allow the clear water's current to pass through your heart, you must stop trying to manipulate the painting by forcing meaning into it.

ು

Eileen, a sturdy, intense woman in her early forties, painted a self-portrait. She painted her body dark red except for round yellow breasts and long white hands. Her purple hair flew wildly in the wind. She called me over.

"I need a check," she said. "I am wondering if I am still coming from my heart. I am totally sure I was before, but now I don't know anymore."

I noticed that Eileen's palette was filled with a big blob of black paint. "What were you going to do with that paint?" I asked.

"I was going to paint two black wings on my body to express the part of me that wants to explore the world!" she answered.

"What question would help you find out if you are coming from your heart, or if the Dragon of Meaning has taken over your inspiration?" I asked.

"If I was going to do something other than the black wings, what would I do?" she said.

"Oh, no. This is not a question to ask. It goes to your head and makes you think even more. It is asking for your opinion. You need to go back to Point Zero and see what happens. Find the judgment that stops you and build your question on it."

"If I stop protecting my feelings, what would I do?" she risked. Nothing moved inside her. She remained silent and tense.

I probed, "Are you really listening inside? You do not have to come up with anything special. Remember it is not about finding something, but about letting it pass through you, out of the depth of your being. You need to go back to a place without expectations," I said. "No need to struggle and force images out."

She listened again to her question, and her face lit up with a whimsical smile. It was as if she had suddenly entered the room. She exclaimed, "Well, I could paint the clan! The . . . clan!"

"What do you mean?" I asked, curious.

Surprised that I didn't understand her, she repeated, "The clan." And with a naked look, she explained, "I would paint my father on the left and my mother on the right of me."

"When you imagine painting, either the black wings or your parents, which one is closer to your heart?"

There was no hesitancy. Eileen was eager to start and motioned for me to leave. A wave of strong feelings passed through her. They tumbled down her lively face, raw and naked, tears and smiles mixed in a touching embrace.

A couple of hours later I met an enthusiastic Eileen on the lunch line.

"Since painting this morning, I have been thinking of Bob

Dylan," she shared with me. Then, without warning, she burst out singing his song "I Shall be Released."

When the desire to paint what has meaning is put aside, feelings wake and travel through the heart.

Omens?

I f anything can be dangerous in painting, it is what you don't paint. It is never what you did paint, no matter how horrid it may seem or if it portrays painful events in your life. *What you paint spontaneously always aims at integration and healing.* Your intuition is not interested in what you know or in what you are afraid of. Its work is a lot more subtle and deep and always tends toward harmony. Negative images are not omens—they do not foretell bad things to come. When you enter the Creative Quest, you are in unfamiliar territory. It has a different language and order of things. The true meaning is not in the content of the images as the Dragon of Meaning wants you to believe. It is in the movement of your creativity that passes through your being. The true meaning is in the process itself.

☙❧

Claudine, a usually very self-confident woman, called me over to her. She was pale and looked at me anxiously when she spoke; her words were hesitant, broken, almost inaudible. I had to ask her to repeat herself.

"It is very difficult for me to paint anything threatening because a few years ago I had breast cancer. When I look at the paintings I did then, I realize that I had painted my breast cancer without even knowing it! I think my unconscious was trying to give me a message because I painted a lot of cells. Now, I am afraid that it is giving me more terrible news, so I am terrorized to go ahead," she confided.

I looked at her painting. A huge beast was lifting its heavy paw toward a young, defenseless woman, herself. Her fearful mind was debating what kind of bad omen it could represent.

"You are truly facing your fears," I commented. "Here is the beast frightening you out of your wits. You, such a courageous woman! Your freedom and spontaneity brought the beast, and now your mind wants to take it back. Your mind is threatened because you are progressing on your Creative Quest.

"A painting would never create something that is not already in your dreamworld. By expressing what comes spontaneously, by allowing what is unconscious to manifest, it becomes accepted, integrated. When a dark event is brought to light, healing can start at levels, emotional, physical, or spiritual, that have not happened yet. Painting would never create a new problem or disease, or simply come to deliver bad news. *Creative energy is benevolent.* It works for harmony and healing. Creativity addresses problems at mysterious levels, and images cannot be taken literally. It is important to trust the healing principle of creation. If not, you lose your capacity to respond spontaneously and truly explore. Can you ask yourself questions to go back to Point Zero and find what to do next? Can you build a question on what stops you?"

"What would I paint if I was not afraid of bringing up bad things on me, or if I didn't read the future in my images?" Claudine asked herself.

She listened carefully to the question. "I got it!" she said and went back to paint the monster's dark paws approaching the woman, now from all sides, a half-dozen of them, black and threatening. She painted without restraint, freeing herself. Letting go of her worries, she had closed the dragon's trap.

"What a powerful process!" she exclaimed with the voice of someone who had just started on an amazing journey.

*Remember, the little voices in your head don't
know what they are talking about.*

Painter's Corner

While you're painting, you may suddenly find yourself in the Painter's Corner. From that place, whether you look right or left, you see only walls. You do not have the slightest idea of what to do next. Discouraged and empty, you feel you have exhausted every possibility. You have reached a dead end. The Painter's Corner appears as a wake-up call. Something inside must shift.

The solution to the corner is not to be found within the corner. Ideas won't help there. There is only one option left if you want to face that place. You must stop looking for the next thing to paint. You need to stop following the threat of your expectations and let go of your desire for special meaning. *What you need is to go back inside yourself and be vulnerable to your feelings.* You need to make a turnaround. Go back to Point Zero, face your dragons, and follow your new inspiration.

The Painter's Corner offers a precious opportunity for depth. It gives you a choice: to listen to its message or to quit painting. If you quit at such a time, it will be very difficult to return.

෨෨

Howard, a serious and determined young man, had dared to come to the workshop even though he had not painted since childhood. He had been looking sad and restless since the workshop began, two days earlier. He had painted little plants in various green colors all over the paper, except for the very center where a small man was lying with a blue blanket covering half his body. He had left a large white space above the man.

"I am not interested in my painting anymore," he told me. "All these detailed plants feel tedious to paint." Then, after a moment, he said, "The only thing I can think of is to paint wide red strokes over everything."

"That would only be relieving physical tension but wouldn't address the true need underneath," I told him. "Can you identify the judgment that is blocking your creativity and pushing you into a corner?"

"I think that *I should* continue painting details on my plants or that *I should* paint larger things to make it more interesting. I guess my question could be, 'What would I do if I didn't have to paint small details or big strokes, if I could let anything else in without worrying about its shape or meaning?'" With that, a shadow passed over Howard's face. "My father passed away recently," he said gravely.

"I am very sorry to hear that," I said. "Could you let yourself feel your feelings?"

"This is my father, here," he said, pointing to the man in the middle of the painting. "I could paint the space above him all black. I have never painted black before."

He did paint black, then he painted little vines moving in and out of the painting for another hour while some of the grief moved through him. Then he turned to me and said with a clear voice, "Feeling is always the answer, isn't it?" and went back to painting a thin ray of sun passing through the lively plants all the way to his father's heart.

Worms and Beauty

A divine fire blazes within you
Don't jump back like a coward
Cook in that fire!
Bake like bread.

R U M I

I had just finished a painting of death when I felt pulled to paint my face in the process of decomposition. (See painting no. 24.) It might look like a morbid subject but that was not my experience. When I painted my face, I actually experienced the worms crawling on my skin. The sluggish, fat, slow-eating gray worms were invading my head, eating me up. Soon, they reached my eyes. Like a child playing with scary things, I wondered how much I could take. I was repulsed and disgusted, but I felt release and excitement at finally facing what I had been unknowingly afraid of my whole life.

The magic of painting seemed to increase my ability to feel extreme and intense feelings. I felt like a child finally free to explore forbidden places, allowed to enter firsthand into an area that had been taboo since birth. I was allowed to let these powerful images out, to expose and explore them. My trust in the creative process was so strong that I felt there was no need to react or worry or even assign special meaning to my images. Pushing these images away would have been an avoidance. Intuition had brought the images, and intuition had its own intelligence and knew what I needed.

I can truly say that, despite the frightening subject, I enjoyed painting those worms. Watching the children paint years ago taught me about following my spontaneous creativity to the end. Children do not have the prejudices and superstitions that adults have. They are born explorers. Every aspect of life interests them. They love to stretch their limits and the intensity of discovery, and so do I.

When the worms appeared in my painting, I felt eager to experience new sensations without succumbing to my fears. It was intense and scary, but an exhilarating adventure, an exploration that had been on hold since childhood. It allowed me to face the reality of death within me. When the worms crawled on me, not only in my eyes but also inside my mouth, I knew deep inside that there was no escaping the truth. I didn't assign meaning to my painting: the feelings were so powerful that words and labels had no place in it.

As I kept painting, the worms approached my heart. A large thick white worm crawled slowly toward its core. I thought I was going to faint. I knew that the moment the big worm entered my heart, death would strike her final blow. When my brush got close, death was no longer a concept but an inescapable fact. I stared into the eye of impermanence. In that instant, I woke up to the fragility of existence, and the immense beauty of life filled me.

6
CREATIVITY
AND
SPIRITUALITY

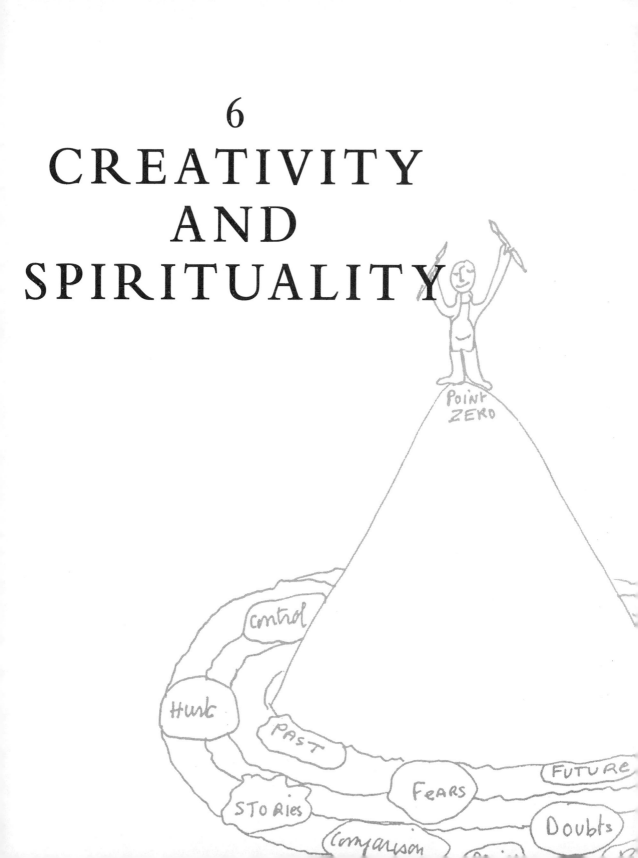

Intuition Moving
Through My Life

Painting has changed my life because it has brought me self-expression, playfulness, and a sense of wonder. With it, intuition has entered my daily living, and I have become acquainted with its mysterious and sometimes puzzling voice.

The continual use of my intuition in painting has taught me to respond to life's demands from a place of feelings and depth rather than from my thinking mind. Intuition has showed me how to *respond* rather than *react*. It has showed me that there is a way around any obstacle and that destruction never works in the long run. From the start of my creative process, I noticed that when I stopped painting and reentered my everyday life, my intuition stayed awake and guided me toward what I truly felt or wanted. It is a little hard to describe, but after painting, I would see things and people differently, and sometimes even the colors and sharpness of the world would stand out in new ways and the sense of my self would be altered.

The more I used my intuition, the more it wanted to be used. The more I listened to it, the more it talked, no matter what activity I was in. In writing, for instance, intuition taught me to be courageous and efficient. When I planned to write a book, the scope of the project weighed heavily on me. I decided to let go of the idea of the finished product and write about only what I was truly interested in, what called me or pushed through me for unknown reasons. Not only did I enjoy the adventure of writing, but I wrote a lot more than I would have and gave my best and deepest to the project until one day there was enough for a book. My intuition had guided me, and my passion wrote the book. Of course, later I had to organize the work and clean it up, but I looked at that as the workmanship phase of the creative process. Every obstacle would stretch my ability to respond creatively and face the unknown as I had done so many times during painting.

When I started painting many years ago, I felt like a second-hand person because I was in touch with myself so little that I had to constantly borrow feelings from other sources to fill the void. I took my political views and ideas on education and arts from friends, magazines, and fashionable speakers. I was stunned when I realized the depth and potential of my own feelings. They were not as simple or as straightforward as I had thought. They blended, often in contradictory ways. They were complex and mysterious and always in flux. Often, they couldn't have been described with one work, but expressed only with paints or poems.

As I developed a relationship with my intuition, I noticed it would manifest as a sensation like a knock at the door of my heart or in the middle of my belly. When I heard the call, I knew I had just to go there. In life, as in painting, intuition would ask me to be open to the unknown, to be willing to feel what I didn't expect, to respond in a new way, often to take risks, or to wait patiently for the right time. Intuition showed me the deadliness of judgments and self-denial and the vital importance of trusting the deep voice of the heart. My intuition was demanding that I be alive with all my might.

I slowly became allergic to boredom and routines. For the first time in my life, I walked out of movies, plays, or lectures if I didn't feel interested. I felt my time was precious, and I didn't want to waste it anymore. Intuition reacquainted me with play. I learned to express my spontaneity wherever I went, whether I was with a group of people or by myself. I learned to bring new elements of play to the most trivial occupation.

Intuition and spontaneity go together. Intuition is the substance, the fuel that creation uses. Spontaneity carries it into the world; it is the spark that lights it. Play, in its pure form, is the manifestation of life. Every human is born with the capacity and the instinct to play. Life wants and needs play. Often adults forget or ignore it, and sadly the faculty atrophies. Children learn and grow through play. For adults, play has a very important function, too. When I play, my thoughts, feelings, and concerns reorganize themselves within a deeper principle: They go back where they truly belong. Pressures and expectations drop because of the freedom of response and the lack of fear of stepping outside the lines. I let go of my grip on things. Play brings laughter, a necessary ingredient to a happy life. Laughing opens wide the windows of the heart.

Intuition also plunged me into the vast mystery of existence. I keep saying that I can never get used to life: too much puzzling unknown, too much to explore. Often, I find myself looking around me and sensing depths of reality within the smallest things. I marvel as if it were my first day on earth. When I am painting, a sense of spirit moves in and out of everything, even when life is complicated and difficult. Intuition taught me that stressful times often announce an opening, a change, a release, and an evolution.

As in painting, I practice not clinging to what appears on the canvas of my life. I go for process, for the experience of living, rather than for the grabbing of a tangible product. I always attempt to face the unknown, to be fully engaged in what I do moment to moment. I know now that to respond from the heart is all that matters.

Reaching the Point of No Return

If you stop asking for what you do not need,
What you need will come to you.

NISARGADATTA MAHARAJ

One of the greatest delights in my teaching career has been to watch my students enter the Point of No Return in their process. The *Point of No Return* is a point at which creative expression has moved to such a deep level that you cannot imagine living without it. You have reached that point when your creativity flows through the different seasons of your process without doubting the purpose or direction of the creative force. No matter if you paint, write, dance, no matter which medium you use, creativity is now part of your life with its playfulness, wisdom, and passion.

The critical mind is the greatest obstacle on your way to the Point of No Return. It doubts, questions, judges, organizes, dissects everything you do. Standing between you and your work, it attempts to control your every move and evaluates your creation inch by inch in terms of success and failure. Its relentless voice makes sweeping statements about your abilities and often presses you to give up or compromise. It pushes you to endlessly fix, repair, change, and cover up. When you are in that mode, spontaneity is not welcome, and the option of taking risks is unlikely chosen, tension builds, and enjoyment flies away.

To reach the Point of No Return, you must have true understanding of the creative process. You must become acquainted and intimate with creativity's purpose and find out how it works. This is the most substantial requirement to reach the Point of No Return. Without understanding, creativity depends on grace or guessing, and its comings and goings can become quite frustrating and widely spread apart.

When you are on your Creative Quest, you may encounter many pitfalls and dragons, but spontaneous learning will develop through practice if you understand the basics principles of creation. Do not be discouraged when something you do not like or do not want happens. The road is tricky because so much conditioning is in the way. Do not think it is only your weakness. You are also experiencing a collective conditioning, a huge cloud hovering above those who enter the creative process—a cloud inherited from generations that have been driven to product rather than process.

You must develop your intuitive strength to move through the different phases that may precede the Point of No Return. Judgments weigh heavy and slow you down from time to time; however, you will feel the exaltation of a moment of freedom and pure creation that first happens one second at a time, then two or three, then a minute or two, and then more and more often for longer periods. Each instant fills your being with precious fuel and brings joy.

When you first take risks by being spontaneous, your critical voices may call your work childish, or cartoonlike, or simply bad. The next phase happens when you become less attached to the result, and the voices say that your painting is without meaning. The critical mind has moved to a more subtle level but is still clinging. This is actually a good sign; a sign that your mind is not controlling what you are doing and that your intuition is becoming stronger than your thoughts. Let the judgments float. Depths are bound to develop from that point on; patterns and beliefs attached to the result are bound to break.

Then, one day, you are lifted up. Your painting seems to paint itself. Blissfully, you paint images and colorful shapes that you could not have imagined. A sense of flow and pure harmony appear that are not attached to the result but to the doing. You have entered creativity *in full bloom*. In that phase, you suddenly discover with certainty that what you think about your painting is irrelevant and subjective. The joy you feel cannot be compared with any other experience; you are moved by a greater force. You become fully present and responsive. This is a pure moment of creation. You know that this force is in your life and you can tap into it from now on. You have reached the Point of No Return. When the bliss ends after a while, since it must follow creative cycles, you do not doubt everything again, but rather feel gratefulness for the gift to create. In that state, you are willing to go through the phases of creativity with curiosity, anticipation, and wonder, but not with fear or worry. You are taken care of. You are in the hands of the Great Painter. In it, there is no return.

Can you hear the call of the unknown?

Insights

I've had many problems in my life,
Most of which never happened.

MARK TWAIN

ntuitive painting stimulates insight. An insight is a spontaneous realization through the heart, a burst of wisdom that
comes directly from intuition. The intelligence of creativity
speaks through insights. It happens in painting when the dreamworld has room to unfold without being manipulated. The dream
images, when expressed consciously, work at a deep level of the
psyche, stirring up truths that had been otherwise ignored or
missed, allowing deep meaning to surface.

Insights carry the *sacred aspect of creation.* Through insights,
true creative energy enters the hidden or ignorant parts of our being, offering its light and wisdom. Often, insights are not connected
with the literal meaning of the painting. They work at the root level.

When an insight appears, the painter often has an urge to share
it because of the beauty of its wisdom and the astonishment of realization. When my students share their insights, they speak with
their whole being. They are living every word they utter and know

them fully, whether they talk about a relationship and the sudden understanding of old patterns or the meaning of their lives as children or about a specific turning point in their lives or about a work situation or their purpose in life.

Sometimes insights fuel metaphysical questions or concerns about creativity and the search for spirit. Larger dimensions and expanded perceptions are part of every insight. When a thing is seen in its totality, seen against the background of life, the truth is bound to rise, whether practical or spiritual. Wisdom is born. When my students share their insights, I can hear their souls rejoice. Insights are food for their Creative Quests.

*The capacity to suddenly see one truth or idea
within the context of the totality of existence
is what creates an insight.*

God or the
Idea of God?

Where is the door to God,
In the sound of a barking dog,
In the ring of a hammer,
In a drop of rain,
In the face of everyone I see.

HAFIZ

J was brought up in a home where God was mentioned only occasionally. I remember my mother telling me, when I was four or five years old, that I should always behave well because God could see everything I was doing. When I grew older, I had no belief in God, even though I had to admit that life was quite mysterious.

One day, when I found myself spontaneously painting God, I was astounded. "Where is this coming from?" I kept wondering. The painting was easy to paint, but my mind was twirling with a million thoughts. I sincerely believed that lightning was going to strike me for so boldly daring to paint such a sacred image. I kept looking around, expecting some terrible consequences for my action. My mind tried to reassure me. "It's all fantasy!" it said, but I was definitively feeling on edge and afraid of my audacity.

Still, I kept painting God and made Him naked. That was even more out of line, a plain sacrilege, but my intuition was pushing me to put more and more details in the painting. I painted people trapped under His legs, and I put myself there, caught in His power. I felt a lot of heat going through me during this process. When I finally finished, I was excited, shaky, and worried.

To my surprise, I instantly felt an urge to paint another painting of God, but this time much bigger. (See painting no. 12.) The new painting was taller than I was. I had to courageously confront God face-to-face while painting it. It took two days to complete and was a very intense and stimulating experience. This painting made me realize that the idea of a frightening and revengeful God was deeply ingrained inside me and had been there without my knowledge.

Suddenly, I had an insight that I had not actually painted a God that I didn't know and didn't believe in. I had painted only a *concept* of God, a concept that was lodged in my mind since childhood. As I painted that fearful idea of God, I became free of it, and experienced God in a completely new way—as an immensely benevolent universal energy and as a vibrant and mysterious presence. That transcendent feeling reached the depths of my heart and soul and transformed my perceptions of life—that God had definitively nothing in common with the old ideas I had inherited from childhood.

That experience brought me an insight about one of the main functions of spontaneous expression. In that process, *painting is a destroyer of concepts*. Painting reveals and breaks concepts to allow the experience of what is unknowingly felt or perceived. Painting had guided me to first face and then to discard my ideas and prejudices about God so I could explore what God truly meant to me. This process had mysteriously released my consciousness from old beliefs, opening the door for the true experience of the sacred.

A Zen Master
in Your Pocket

I am not I
I am this one
Walking beside me whom I do not see,
Whom at times I manage to visit
And at other times I forget.

JUAN RAMÓN JIMÉNEZ

Self-confidence in creation comes from realizing that you always know the next step; somewhere inside you, you know as a fact that the information is there. Then, you only need try different questions until one clicks you open. A Zen master is always hiding somewhere close, ready to wake you up, to throw you back into the wilderness of your Creative Quest by bringing you to the essential truth. The hidden weapon against lethargy and habits might just be hiding in your very pocket. The wisdom of the Zen master is at reach of hand.

☙❧

Suzie, a young and lively woman, had been painting slowly and steadily for a few hours. She was nervously chewing gum. Her painting showed a tall yellow building with rows of square windows, a woman behind it, waving her hand, and a huge purple cat crawling on a red street.

"Do you know what makes you want to chew gum?" I asked.

"Yes, to release tension. If not, I would have to go to the chiropractor because my joints would hurt!" she answered matter-of-factly.

"Do you think it would be possible to express and release these feelings of tension through painting?" I asked.

"I tried already, but it doesn't work," she replied.

"What kind of question do you need to ask yourself in order to paint from the whole of you? Right now, you have fragmented yourself. There is the one who is chewing gum and there is the one who is painting. To create is to respond fully from your whole being. The desire to chew gum is a pointer. It is trying to force your attention where you need it."

In a dull, contracted voice, Suzie asked herself, "What would I do if I could let myself paint anything?" but the question didn't bring any response.

"What question could work for you? What would bring you back to Point Zero, the place of no preference? You need to build your question with the block itself. You need to give yourself permission to be nervous and to feel," I told her.

Always up for a challenge, she thought hard for a while, going in, searching.

"What would I paint if I was not afraid to be even *more* nervous?" and abruptly added, "What is it that *I'd rather not* paint?" Her eyes suddenly lit up; I could see her curiously watching her painting as if something was happening on it.

"I would put dark, thick liquid coming out of the windows and the roof and the sky and dripping over there and . . . here . . .

and . . . here . . . I am going to do it!" she cried, relief written on her face.

When I returned a few minutes later, Suzie came really close to me. With a wide smile, she opened the bulging pocket of her apron to show me what was there. I was amazed to discover in it a huge assortment of multicolored sticks of gum of various sizes.

"Next time I reach for one, I will know what is happening," she said, with a sparkle of humor in her eyes. "The gum will remind me that I am not painting with my whole self!"

"Yes," I said, "you are very lucky; you have a Zen master in your pocket!"

Meeting
the Spirit

When one sense perceives the hidden
The invisible world becomes apparent to the whole.

RUMI

When you enter creation deeply, a surrendering of your will happens. You don't insist anymore that you know what needs to happen better than the movement of your intuition. You truly let go of the direction and content of your work and welcome the mysterious unknown. In such a receptive state, the voice of the spirit and its archetypes may surface in your consciousness and paint themselves in front of your astonished eyes. Your creative process reconnects you with a hidden and expanded reality. This transcendent experience is a confirmation of the force of spirit that passes through the human heart when it is given room.

Sharon, a sensitive, artistic woman, was painting a picture of St. Francis, larger than life. He was wearing a long indigo robe with a coarse belt and was standing against a soft yellow background. His face was left undone. From his open sleeves, Sharon was attempting to paint his hands, but she became disturbed and just couldn't do it.

"What do I do?" she asked. "Should I force myself to paint the hands? Should I interpret the discomfort as a message not to? Does it mean that I should leave St. Francis with no hands?" she asked with some disbelief.

"Your mind cannot answer these questions because it does not understand what is outside itself! Intuition comes from another place," I told her. "Two possible things may be happening. One, your intuition for some mysterious reason does not want you to paint hands. Or, two, you are not inwardly ready to paint them. In that case, an inner process is happening that needs to complete itself for the hands to appear. In any case, you must wait and do what the process needs for it to mature. Then, painting the hands will flow effortlessly if they are meant to be. The garden of your dreamworld fosters many seeds. Each has its own timing and rhythm. Don't stop. Go somewhere else; find what must be done in the meantime."

Hesitantly, Sharon asked herself, "What does the painting need?"

"Oh, no! That question is too protective and directed. You are asking the painting for a logical answer even though you may need something unreasonable, something well beyond your expectations. Remember, you are dealing with the dreamworld. You are in the land of the Creative Quest; you are in a fantastic place filled with dragons and mysteries. Do not bring your work back to a mundane, matter-of-fact level. Can you find another question using the block you are experiencing now?"

Sharon tried again. "What would I paint next if it was okay for St. Francis to have hands or no hands and I didn't have to worry about it?" she asked, and her reply came quickly. "I would paint a bird on the side of his head! It has long feathers, and it's gray. I would rather have it in red tones, but no, it's gray!" she said, already roaming her dreamworld.

Sharon painted the bird on the right and a sad-looking face on the left. All of a sudden, she felt drawn to paint St. Francis's long hands in flesh tones. It happened like magic. This is when the astonishment set in: The hands had stigmata, the crucifixion wounds of Christ. This vision brought Sharon such bewilderment that it became obvious to her what had kept her from painting the hands at first.

The creative process is alive, and its heart beats in unison with the painter's. Intuition is always aware of the deeper levels of feelings and perceptions. The image of the stigmata had been forming and maturing in Sharon during her uncertainty. Forcing what was not ripe could have made her lose touch with the depth of the process.

Sharon, now one with her painting, had entered another world. The door to her soul had suddenly opened, and she had met the vast mystery of her own spirit. With astonished reverence, she painted the sacred wounds, with drops of the blessed blood running all the way to the floor.

"I didn't know such an experience could occur in painting," she shared later. "I understand a lot more about the power of the creative process after what happened to me this afternoon." Then, with a tremor of wonderment in her voice, she added, "Spirit filled me."

Creativity is the messenger of the spirit. Its messages wake up the soul, for each in a unique way.

Natural Wisdom

All my skill and poetry
Fit into a single cup
Unless the wine comes from the beloved
I will not drink a sip of it.

RUMI

here are seeds of wisdom in everyone. All of the wisdom of the world is there. This wisdom is not the kind you find in ideas or in books. It is a natural, deeper, more integral wisdom, a garden of precious seeds that lies at the core of your being, waiting to bloom.

Traditional wisdom, on the other hand, is made up of ideas and principles that accumulate coming from an outside source, which communicates and explains them. These ideas are received by the mind first, hoping to be integrated and used later. Natural wisdom does not deal with the mind in that way; it is born spontaneously in the depth of the being. When an experience or a perception is finally understood, it is a discovery that is bound to have great impact because it comes directly from the meeting of your whole being with universal energies. Intuitive creation stimulates the birth of natural wisdom because it puts old beliefs and patterns out of the way, allowing you to see with new eyes.

❦

Annie suddenly felt an overwhelming desire to paint the crucifixion. It startled her since she was not interested in the Christian tradition. But having learned to trust the intuitive process, she went ahead and started painting. First in the middle of the space, she painted Christ on a wooden cross. She worked in a sort of peaceful trance and with great concentration.

"There is so much coming to me, so fast, I barely have the time to keep up with it," she said, amazed by the appearance of what seemed an endless flow of images, all bursting with substance.

On the right of the cross, she painted a smaller cross and planted the nails on her own body, and on the left, another cross with a red swollen heart at the center.

"It is like stepping through a door and finding a whole other reality that exists with all its details, waiting to be painted," she said, looking at me with wide eyes, utterly surprised, almost in shock. "A moment before, I had no idea it was all there," she added.

On the bottom of the paper, Annie painted a half-earth with her family home in soft blue and, behind it, steep brown mountains covered with pine trees. Then snow started to fall. "I can feel the snowflakes on my face as I am doing it," she said. She had entered into her painting without resistance, her familiar reality was dissolving, and new worlds were opening, bombarding her with new sensations and perceptions.

Then, a deep, dark canyon flowed with swift waters between two mountains. The most miniscule details took shape—sharp angled rocks, dark cracks, rich-green vegetation, animals grazing, and even tiny insects. Then, at last, stars and lights burst from the sky.

"All of a sudden, I understand the meaning of the crucifixion!" she exclaimed as she turned toward me and looked into my eyes with the intensity of somebody who just had a revelation.

"Oh, it is quite different from what I always thought. I believed it meant to show us the path of martyrdom, that it exemplified suffering. But no, I see it now. It expresses that what is being crucified is only temporary, the man-made story of who we think we are, our self-image, our personality, the holding on, the clinging, the limitations. What is crucified is what does not really exist, what has no real substance. It tells us, 'Look, only the spirit is real; do not be afraid; let go of appearance; let go of your little self; come, melt with me. The real substance, the spirit is untouchable.' See the beauty of that."

In awe, I listened to Annie, witnessing the birth of natural wisdom born directly from a depth of experience in her heart.

When the experience of creation is complete, when intuition is fully listened to, wisdom will rise. This is because wisdom is born in the truth of what is fully perceived. Intuition opens the heart; wisdom is the fragrance of a feeling heart. There is no other way to contact wisdom than by letting things be as they are and letting them move you. When truth stirs up, you perceive life differently, insights jump into your life, the unthought meets you, and you find yourself in the middle of being and knowing. When wisdom lets itself be known to you through process, it is fully your own; you do not need explanations, justifications, or examples. It falls into your heart like a fully ripe fruit that has grown its own sweetness under the sun and the rain. *Your wisdom is custom-made for your soul,* custom-made! It fits perfectly, nothing needs to be added to it. Born in you, wisdom infuses your whole being. This is the transformative power of creation. It touches everything in you, your heart, your mind, your body; it touches that place where everything meets inside: a place that has no holes. It tells us: Stop listening out there. The real meaning of everything is inside, and no one or nothing else can find it for you.

Instead of staying in the little schoolhouse where you learn only what others have learned, what has been passed down and recycled many times, you move out and leave that enclosed space. You find out that you can encounter the new directly and that your vehicle is your own creative power. When you enter the simple act of creation, the wall cracks and you walk through. You then realize that nothing is missing. To practice painting is to practice "nothing is missing." You let colors, images, and shapes emerge from your brush; nothing is missing. That is enough to rejoice.

The painting is the fire. In the forest some seeds need fire to crack open—a fire that burns the walls of separation between what you think you know and what you really know, between your thinking habits and your own natural wisdom.

Suddenly,
Two Worlds

*A mysterious wind comes by
And moves the invisible.*

RUMI

As soon as I put my paintbrush on the white surface, I knew I was not going to paint a human body. For the first time, I was pulled to paint a universal being. I made it blue with traces of red and yellow, each half of its eyes a different color. The turbulent red river of life passed through its chest. In it, people from time past, present, and to come flowed with the current til infinity. I painted myself there; I was but a tiny drop.

When I finished painting the river of people, my small studio was suddenly filled with a crowd of mysterious presences from a reality unknown to me. There was now not one but two worlds—my familiar world and another mysterious world. Both were fully real and present, superimposed on each other. I was awed by what I saw and felt. I proceeded immediately to paint that other world filled with strange blue beings floating in space. (See painting no. 22.)

Through that crack in my perception, I realized how little I knew. Where was I? Who was I? There was so much I could no longer ignore. Painting carried me to another state of consciousness, and to my astonishment, it had opened my eyes to new dimensions of seeing. In a fraction of a second, my familiar perceptions had been pushed away as surely as if I had woken up from a dream. I went back to paint with renewed passion, eager to delve deeper into my quest.

Creative passion is a place of astonishment.

The Eye-Eating
Buddha

Your duty is to be;
And not to be this or that.
RAMANA MAHARSHI

As artists, we often want to feel special. We want to be recognized for our work. Our greedy egos love to accumulate medals and proof of originality and depth. Art is a land of temptation because in it everything is personal, unique, and prone to the admiration of others. We have to tread the ground of creativity very carefully not to be caught in these ego traps. If we fall into a trap, we miss the best part of creation: the exploration into the mystery of life and spirit.

One day, while painting Buddha, I noticed that he would promptly eat anything I released from my self-centeredness and selfishness. He never seemed to tire of eating bits of my ego, no matter how small. I laughed hard when I finally understood why Buddha had such a big round belly. (See painting no. 39.) Buddha's belly has absorbed large quantities of worldly eyes, eyes full of greed, envy, pride, attachments, and projections; the eyes of super-

Ego Trap

ficiality. I soon realized that Buddha was a great companion to the painter because what prevents pure creation is attachment. As soon as anything product-oriented becomes a little loose, it is quickly sucked into Buddha's stomach. It is a precious help to artists on the Creative Quest when they are lost or distracted by the weight of expectations and petty motives. Committed painters discover that their creative powers are stimulated and enhanced as Buddha's hungry mouth eats their egotistic desires. The constant devouring of our old ways of seeing and doing is an invaluable gift.

Buddha always points to freedom from self-identification and to the discovery of a life free from attachment. Attachment, however subtle, is the target of his work as well as the main obstacle on the journey to creativity. Attachment relentlessly pursues artists on their quests, invading their hearts and minds, narrowing or even destroying their creative paths. The tempting promise of a beautiful or spiritual painting seems to dangle in front of them. These prizes are, of course, a mirage. The moment they reach to grab one, it vanishes. These desired products have no real substance in the world of being and have the unfortunate power to end the Creative Quest.

Buddha, the emptier, the great dissolver, eats your unnecessary tendencies to own and use everything—if you let him. He laughs because, despite the apparent drama, an enjoyable play is going on.

There is humor in the schism:
Between worldly eyes and all-encompassing eyes
Between painting from intuition or from mind's corner
Between a state of being and a state of thinking
Between now and now
Between what can be seen and what is perceived
Between the idea of a past and the idea of a future

Buddha, the eye-eater, the painter's guardian, rejoices at the great theater of life, the majestic play of the human race. He laughs at the dance of form and no form while fattening his belly.

I remember the first time I heard Buddha's laugher. I had been lying in bed, sick for a few days, when suddenly I heard it. I got up, instantly called to paint. I realized then that I didn't have to take myself so seriously or look at my life in such a narrow context. The laughter pointed at cracks in my consciousness, inspiring me to let go of the stereotypes that projected the same blueprints everywhere I looked and to let go of thinking the same thoughts.

I let my intuition guide me, and I started laughing, too. Between my thoughts and beliefs were dimensions I could not have dreamed of. The greatest surprise was to discover a security there that I could not have imagined, a background of meaning. It was not dependent anymore on a little stash of truths and accomplishments I had accumulated. It was found beyond all things, in what lies at the edge of the universe, in that place I searched as a child, right at the edge of matter, a place of spirit.

My intuition, I realized, had been trying to guide me there my entire life. I had not been listening. It was time to finally look from inside, to use other eyes. The knock on the door was too loud. The spirit in me was too hungry. I surrendered to my creativity, and my brush found the other place, the place of great undoing as easily as a bird follows its instinct home. Within moments, I was painting again while Buddha chewed on my old eyes.

The Ecstasy
of Painting

The possibilities of painting are immense. Creativity opens a vast world of experiences that feeds the soul much beyond our knowledge. A well of archetypes awaits the artist on a Creative Quest and is revealed at the most unexpected moment and in the most unforeseen ways.

Intuitive creation puts in motion a process that reaches deep into the psyche and explores different levels of consciousness. At times, it delves into out-of-the-ordinary perceptions and reveals what usually escapes our main senses. This amazing process functions naturally and is always present when intuition is at work. It delivers insights, visions, or realizations, depending on what concepts are being broken or what truths are being revealed. The full impact of a realization cannot be rushed. When the mind starts to jump ahead, to grab meaning, or to force the painting into a particular direction, the realization withdraws and stays out of reach until interference stops.

Every so often, painting brings an experience that reaches the mind through insight or revelation *as it is being painted.* One day, I suddenly started painting Christ dancing on my body. I felt so full inwardly that I found myself falling in ecstasy. I could sense with perfect clarity the sacred feet of Christ dancing upon my body and squeezing out drops of truth. It was a moment of pure joy and harmony among my painting, my experience, and me. Buried resistances, hidden feelings, and spiritual perceptions were touched at their core all the way to my soul. They were the focus of the loving feet of this great Master. In His dance, Christ woke them from their long sleep and gently, swiftly activated them.

I became aware of the depth of the help offered. I saw the immensity of my clinging to my work, my life, and my thoughts. I felt that nothing less than the feet of Christ could release some of this attachment. My creativity had unknowingly called this most magnificent spirit. The dance was a great undoing, an unclogging, and an activation of potential awareness. The dancing Christ, in all His love, was catalyst and teacher.

When we create spontaneously, we are held in the amazing power that looks for harmony and happiness. That power activates the ancient longing to rejoin the spirit and to go back to a place before the separation of mind and spirit took over. Every time intuition is used, the spirit dance starts, and with it the love of the universe mends the soul.

The Shift

The One that cannot be found
He is the One I am looking for.

RUMI

I long for something unknown. How do I go about pursuing a search for what I cannot even imagine? Pulled by this mysterious call, craving for something undefinable, I try all paths available to me without success. What do I do next? I realize that what I am looking for cannot be found in the usual ways and in familiar places. Something needs to shift. I have no choice but to generate new eyes for myself, new ways of exploring. I must go where expectations and beliefs are absent, and I must leave my personal history and knowledge of life behind.

There is no known easy switch to other states of being. But the magic is simple. Because I don't control creation, I can use creation to guide me to the edge of the known, all the way to the door of my longing. This is the function of creation. Creative energy works to reunify what is fragmented, to bring the lover back to her love, to infuse the universal in the personal. When the shift happens, new perceptions infiltrate the familiar world, transforming it. Freeing that creative force can open indescribable dimensions of being and perceiving.

The personal self always looks for what resembles it because it is all it knows. It has no means to transcend on its own. It turns in circles, slightly altering things or, at best, recycling old materials. Creativity looks for what is not known, beyond all imagination and stories. There is deep meaning to Rumi's quote:

The One that cannot be found
He is the One I am looking for.

Rumi stresses that we are not merely searching to meet the hidden in us and to explore our inner world. We are longing for the background of existence, the great mystery of life, for the "One that cannot be found." The treasure, the source of longing, cannot be found by the one that is searching for it. Looking at it with worldly eyes makes it disappear instantly. But when the longing unifies with the active surrendering to intuition, we are brought to the door that leads to the mysterious spirit.

To find what cannot be found, we cannot take our usual selves with us; we leave them floating on the ocean of the known world. Only the heart can meet the "One that cannot be found." It is the way of passion to use only the heart in the search for the great unknown and to let intuition be the guide. Nothing fake or superficial will survive the fire of the great unknown, which is fueled by creativity. It burns what touches it, burns the conceptual form of the person, the form that is searching, the form that wants to get something for itself. It burns everything but the heart.

The shift is the passage through creativity to a different level of reality. Or maybe it is an initiation into new perceptions. When we stop questioning the wisdom of our own intuition and master the purity and impeccability of our responses in creation, the shift happens. Then our minds can encompass different times and spaces and go to the edge of form without withdrawing. The sense of spirit becomes a reality. Form and formlessness become two aspects of experience and existence.

7
POINTERS

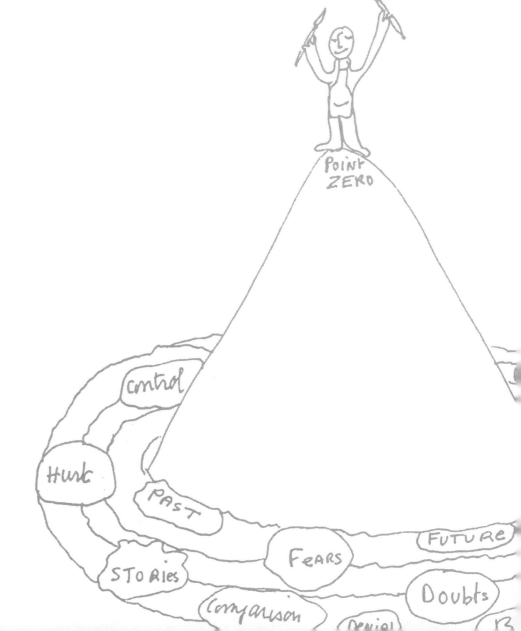

POINT ZERO

control

Hurt

PAST

STORIES

Fears

Comparison

FUTURE

Doubts

Denial

The Ten Principles
of Creativity

1 • Creativity is not sourced by the individual.
Creativity arises out of the energy of the entire universe.

2 • Creativity is part of nature.
Creativity has the liveliness and intelligence of nature.

3 • Creativity is benevolent.
Creativity is unifying and harmonizing. Its mends and heals
what stands in its path. It breaks down and defeats the false and
the unnecessary.

4 • Creativity manifests through intuition and spontaneity.
Trust your intuition and spontaneity. They are the means to
express what is authentic. Every seed brings forth its own fruit.

5 • Each creation is unique.
Don't judge or compare. Every creation in the universe is unique.

6 • Each creation deserves respect.
Respect what you have created, what has come to life. Care for
it. Don't destroy it.

7 • Creativity moves in cycles.

Welcome your natural rhythm. Creation moves with the seasons of your process like everything else in nature—days, seasons, tides, and the lives of plants and planets.

8 • Each creation must be completed.

Finish what you start. Every plant will give its own seed in time. Every painting well completed will bring forth the next one.

9 • Beauty is truth.

Paint with integrity. Do not interfere. Beauty is harmony between you and what you do.

10 • Creativity leads to spirit.

Explore the unknown. Creation leads you to the longing of your heart and soul. Every stream flows toward the ocean.

Love your blobs

Teachings
to Remember

Counting Your Interest

"I don't know if I want to have a lotus floating on my pond or a man and a woman half-immersed in it. What should I do?"

One quick way to answer that question is by asking: *"Inside me, how much do I want to do it on a scale from one to ten?"* Doing it, of course, is not for the result but for the doing. Then, pick the one with the highest number. Never pick anything under six.

Doing Less

Annie had painted dozens of scenes in one painting. "I am getting really tired," she said. "My painting will never be finished. It's endless."

You don't have to paint every image that comes to you. Go to the most crucial, the most vibrant. No need to paint as much as possible in every small place left. Finishing a painting does not mean squeezing five more paintings into it. Finishing is simply going more deeply into what you already have and being open to the unexpected.

I Have No Idea What to Do Next!

"I have tried everything. I can't come up with anything!"

Here is a powerful but simple remedy: Take a brush, put paint on it, any color that comes to you for no reason. *Go to your painting and see if your brush wants to paint, not you.* Don't force it. If it refuses to paint, go and get another color. Do that a few times with a few different colors. What you paint could be something very small, even a dot. Do it for a few minutes until the flow is reestablished.

Your Painting Has Its Own Life

Dane had painted carefully two large bodies. Then he painted wide red strokes over the whole picture. "I think I am done," he said.

"What happened?" I asked. "Why did you cover up such refined work?"

"I didn't know what to do and the color felt good so I used it."

It's not enough to feel good with a color. *You cannot treat your painting as if nothing was on it.* You must respect what has happened before, or your intuition will shut off. Your painting is not a blank space. It has its own life; it deserves respect and care. You must find ways to be free, wild, or daring *without denying* what is already there.

Resolving Your Problems

"Before I came to the workshop, I told my husband that it was harder for me not to come than to come," Liza said. "I just lost my aunt a few months ago. She was like a mother to me. I know I have to paint my feelings about that."

Painting is not about resolving a painful event, even though healing is bound to happen in the process. Painting is a celebration of life, an opportunity to express and play using the whole of you, including the grief and the joy and the curiosity and the big unknown of your life. *Don't limit creativity to one feeling or one emotional event,* no matter how strong it is. *Let life do the healing* through the creative force. Let intuition choose your images.

Dancing on Your Painting

"I got very nervous," said Ilana. "I had to put details on all my trees because after making them on one, I thought I had to do it on all of them." She pointed to a cluster of birch trees in her painting. "I forced myself to do it!"

There is *nothing that you have to do,* ever. If something feels tedious or boring, don't do it. If its need is to be painted, the desire and energy to do it will come back at a later time. Then, you will be inspired and happy to do it. Trust the intelligence of creativity that guides your desires. That intelligence will find a way to complete what needs to be completed. Move from place to place. Dance on your painting. Do what has energy first.

Bringing Out Taboos

"I painted a couple of years ago and it was painful," Carl said. "I haven't painted since then. I didn't want to come to your workshop, but my friend dragged me here. I know painting is about bringing out taboos, and it's hard."

Where did he get that idea? *Creative expression is not about bringing out taboos,* and it is not about resolving problems or following agendas. However, painting *is* revealing. How can it not be? To create is to respond to life passing through you, to respond spontaneously, whether light or dark, obvious or repressed, known or unknown. It is never about following *a set road* and certainly not a limited technique of destroying taboos.

Expressing Darkness

"I have painted a lot of blood in my painting. That really disturbs me, and it disturbs me even more that I enjoyed doing it and did a lot of it. What's wrong with me?"

When expression comes out, it embraces both sides of duality. Do not interpret your painting. You felt good doing it because it was needed. Treat your images like a child at play. *Give yourself permission for anything. No need to worry.* No need to be so serious. You are in the hands of the benevolent energy of creation. No matter what you paint, the alchemy of creation moves its healing power. The only dangerous thing is what you *don't* paint. What you don't paint stays inside you and keeps turning round and round.

Inventing as You Paint

"I want to paint a big eagle, but I don't know how to do it. I don't know in which direction to paint the wings so it will fly!"

Don't visualize the image in advance. Invent it as you go along. Painting is a *moment-to-moment* response. Let your instinct paint the eagle. Get out of your own way. Experiment, play, and trust. You will paint your own unique eagle, not a photograph or a reproduction. You must paint from the inside. The most important part will be what is not expected. The unique qualities will be what does not match the standard eagle and your expectations

Don't Make Resistance the Bad Guy

"I felt bored and without energy a while ago, but I kept painting. I am feeling a little better now. I thought I was going through resistance and should push through. I forced myself, but it was difficult."

Why did you keep painting if you felt bored? *Boredom has its own wisdom.* Listen to it. Resistance is a bell ringing for change. Remember that you are always interested in something, but it may not be what you expect and is often unknown. Search for it. Questions will help you find what really interests you. Take a turn. No need to push and force what resists.

Choosing Options

Steve was extremely sensitive to composition and colors. "I don't know whether or not I should paint an orange line going toward the womb," he said.

Do you ever need to make that kind of choice? Do you think you have to decide? If you think so, you have not sufficiently searched within. *Deep down, there is really only one option.* Your intuition will tell you exactly what to do. Use the questions to discover what's next. Get out of the driver's seat and let the flow of creation pass through you endlessly.

Crossing the Lines

Gene had just painted a city of high-rise buildings under a heavy gray sky. He had painted one of the buildings on fire. "Now I feel like burning the whole city," he said. "Is it okay or is it sick?"

How many times do children paint fire or wars or monsters? They don't become violent by painting such images; on the contrary, painting helps them relieve pressures and express feelings; it helps them grow up and explore. Is it different for an adult? Do you think you are too old to have that freedom? Why take it so literally? Daring your images to appear will free you. What you paint has nothing to do with what you would do in real life. In fact, *it is what is not expressed* that has the potential to lead to strange behavior and violence. It's what happens inside you that is important, not what occurs on your painting.

Going with the Energy

"I am going to paint on the chest of the gold woman because I feel there is no energy there."

Do you think you know better than your intuition what you

need to do next? Intuition uses energy to guide you. If a place does not evoke any response, it means it is not ripe yet or that it does not need anything. *Go where your energy calls,* not your thoughts. If you have a reason to do something, it's not spontaneous.

Compromising Your Intuition

"I painted a mermaid because I didn't know how to paint the legs in that position and there was very little room for them anyway."

There is *never a need to compromise* with your intuition. Compromising may discourage or even shut it off. Stop looking for clever ideas to avoid doing what seems hard to do. Be more humble. Take chances. Invent. Welcome challenges.

Trusting Your Inspiration

"I think my painting is beautiful," Donna said with wonder, looking at her five-foot-long painting of a bouquet of flowers and detailed faces. "I feel like putting color on the faces, but I am afraid I'll mess it up."

You don't need such a dilemma. Do you think your intuition is going to make you do something that does not belong there or that you won't be able to do? Do you think that the intuition that births your painting is going to make you ruin it? You must learn to take risks. With the freedom to invent, you will discover how to paint your images in your own way if you stay in touch with your feelings.

Don't Take It Literally

"I want to paint black crows picking at my mother's head. But I feel it would be wrong. I really love my mother. I am afraid that if I do it I am being a bad daughter. What should I do?"

You must give yourself the freedom to do what comes spontaneously. Feelings are never as simple as they appear. They are complex and often contradictory. Do not try to categorize them. *Let the images come and go and mix in irrational ways.* You are painting your dreamworld. Your black birds are mysterious. An opening is taking place, a freeing and a release of pressure. Enjoy the play and its surprise. You are on your Creative Quest. By the end, you will likely feel more love for your mother, not less.

Painting the First Images

"I painted a street because it came to me when I looked at the blank space. It has been hard from the beginning. I am not feeling very interested in it. What happened?"

The first image often comes from the mind flashing some stored memory, a mind attached to results and looking for a clever or acceptable idea. Real images are often buried and require a little probing and digging into the depths of your being. True images are not interesting little ideas. They are raw; they have a bold power and rise from the belly when you let yourself be vulnerable. *Don't grab the first thing* that comes to your mind unless your energy vibrates with it.

Instant Pudding

"I want intensity now; I don't want to wait. How do I find it?"

You want to arrive at the top of the mountain, but you don't want to climb! Creation is a complete experience with many phases and cycles. Each painting is a journey, a pilgrimage into your heart and soul. No quick fix! No instant pudding! Everything is made from scratch.

Built-in Surge Protector

"After finishing these black holes in the bodies, I painted white ones, and as I did them, I felt a jolt of energy in me. I was thrown into an altered state. I am afraid I have stretched myself too far."

Enjoy the experience and the new energy flowing through you, creating new passageways. Don't worry. When you paint spontaneously, your consciousness allows only as much as you can take. Your *surge protector* is built in.

Not Being Consistent: Creator Privilege

Jane had painted the torso of a woman with a pale blue heart. "I am stuck," she said. "I can't think of anything else, except for painting long fingers holding the woman's heart. But it is not consistent with the rest of my painting. What should I do?"

You never have to follow a subject, a topic, or a theme. It's your privilege as a painter to go with your intuition no matter how inconsistent it seems. It's important to allow what does not fit because it's coming from very deep inside and opens dimensions of feelings you couldn't imagine.

Block or High Altitude?

"I am afraid I have lost my way. I am painting slowly and heavily. I feel I am going through mud."

Don't label every experience a creative block. Creation moves through all kinds of terrain. You may be somewhere in a high altitude, getting used to the lack of oxygen. *If you are neither bored nor tired, keep painting.* The different states are part of the journey. You are a pioneer of your own dreamworld and are exploring remote and hidden areas. A few changes of climate and sensation are to be expected.

Creative Cycles

"What I have been painting has been very deep and inspiring this last week. Now I am painting some stupid little yellow flowers. I think that I have regressed. Am I losing my edge?"

Don't be so hard on yourself. Your creative process is moving through its cycles. After a great expansion, it needs to contract a little to gather its momentum again. It is like going back to base camp to get ready for the next expedition.

The Appearance of Meaning

"I have finished my painting. It shows how the feminine and the masculine balance each other. Now, it's done."

You have been seduced only by the *appearance* of meaning. Images are fooling your mind, giving it the illusion of control. It's a disguise. When you paint from intuition, the deep meaning is never written on the outside of the package.

Being Disconnected

"I am feeling totally disconnected from what I am doing, totally lost," Sharon said, staring at her half-done painting.

Good! It means that your mind is no longer able to hold on to its old rules and patterns. Confusion is a *necessary transition* toward new ways of perceiving. Don't fight it. It will lead you to greater creativity.

Where Are They Coming From?

"I can't paint the hands I saw appearing on the side of my painting because I don't know where they are coming from."

You never have to know where images are coming from. Remember, your intuition paints the unknown. The less you know, the more deeply you enter your dreamworld.

Taste It

"I thought of painting green waters coming out of the rocks, but I am not sure; maybe they are blue or even black. Which color is from my mind?"

If you cannot clearly read your intuition, do a little and see *how it feels to do it* without worrying about how it will look. Taste it; feel it in your body.

If You Put Food on Your Plate, Eat It

"My painting is too big. I thought it would be nice to have all this space. But now I can't face it; it's too much."

You don't need to keep guessing what would happen if you didn't have so much space. Face the discomfort and see what comes out of it. Learn from what is there. To create is to *respond to what you have, not to what* you wish you had. If you put food on your plate, eat it!

A Miserable Sheet of Paper

Annie was squinting and straining, trying to figure out what to think about her painting and how to make it better. "I don't know what to do to make it look more real," she said.

What is all this concern about rendering? What is more important, what is happening on a *miserable* sheet of paper or your life with its freedom of expression? It's astonishing how quickly we forget about what is truly important. Watch out for the trap of product: It may close in on you before you have time to spot it.

Tampering with Nature

"I painted a woman with yellow breasts, but then I felt they were too small. So, I went ahead and painted them bigger. It didn't feel good."

Images are born the way your intuition intended. To interfere and make them fit a certain mold is to tamper with nature. Interfering can never be fulfilling because it's going against the harmony of creation.

Painting the Inside

"I just painted my body with these white balls underneath. I want to fill them in later, but I am not sure with what."

Why do you think something should be inside them? Sometimes there is nothing inside. Leave your options open.

I Don't Like the Way It Looks at Me

"I have painted a volcano erupting and I enjoyed it. Then I saw an eye appearing in the dark sky. I didn't paint it because I didn't like the way it was looking at me."

You paint to express yourself, not to secure a little pleasure. Creation is motivated by truth and mystery. If you overprotect your work, there is no room for genuine inspiration. Be intrigued. Be curious. Nothing bad can come out of an honest response to your intuition. No matter what you paint, creation is *benevolent*. Under every little fear, there is a revelation, an insight, waiting to happen. Let your creation bite you with its truth. It will break your crust.

Looking Is Grabbing

"I keep getting stuck. What am I doing wrong?"

Did you notice your tendency to look at your painting after every stroke and study the effects and endlessly wonder if you like it or not? Every time you look and go back to your head and judge, you are stopping the flow of your intuition. Looking is *grabbing*. There is no freedom as long as you hold on to anything. You can't swim as long as you hold on to the shore. Paint and let go.

Painting the Expected

"I finished painting a big blue cross. I think I should paint a woman on it or maybe a bird being crucified. I want to be really creative and not paint the expected, like Christ."

The fact that you have some choices proves you are in your head. Why not paint Christ if that is what came to you? Simple and obvious images may be very powerful. Each one of us carries all the archetypes of the world in our consciousness. You are being over-zealous and are losing touch with your intuition if you purposely avoid the expected.

Looking at Paintings

I just received a phone call from my friend who had participated in my last workshop. He said, "I was very surprised when I looked at my paintings a few weeks after the workshop. They look so different from what I felt when I was struggling with the patterns."

The way we look at our paintings changes all the time. It is quite important not to take seriously what you think about your painting. In time, the heart sees it without evaluation or analysis.

The Beauty of the Unwanted

"I painted a self-portrait, which I liked doing. Then, the image of my grandmother kept appearing behind me. I don't want to paint her. What should I do?"

What you think is unwanted may pour through your brush with ease. Let it be; let it pass; let it float on the stream of your creativity. Trust the depth of the unwanted. The so-called unwanted mends opposites, reveals the hidden, and reconciles you with yourself. It melts away fear and sets you free because it shows you that there is no need to protect your painting against yourself.

Colors, Abstracts, and Preferences

The first time I looked at the long painting table in the children's studio, which held twenty-four colors, I instantly hated lime green and pink. I couldn't imagine ever using those colors or anybody else wanting to use them. They felt so ugly. To be so strongly repelled by colors is proof of how deeply they affected me. It took many months before I could use lime green, but when I did, it was a powerful experience. Using it threw me into the exploration of a brand-new feeling. I had to admit that no other color could have replaced lime green. At other times, I would love colors so much that I couldn't help but touch them with my fingers and paint with them. Sometimes I wished I could have eaten the colors!

The mind does not really know how to think about colors. Each color contains a unique vibrancy and a power that talk to the senses in deep and mysterious ways. Theories or systems cannot really bind them; they belong to the soul. Colors are alive within you! This is why, through them, you can travel with delight around the maze of the senses and explore unknown lands to the farthest reaches of your consciousness.

When you paint from intuition, images and abstract shapes rise spontaneously and take on colors of their own. I have always enjoyed creating non-representative shapes and letting them evolve inch by inch into a mysterious presence. I think my intuition loves mixing images and abstract because most of my paintings have both. Images carry the content of the dream and its precious power. Abstract shapes enter the unknown; their non-verbal qualities explore a different side of the mystery. Abstract shapes lead to a place *before* the birth of the image. When painting, the combination of abstract forms and images is most natural and allows deep levels of expression. A most intriguing dance takes place between the content and the abstract because of their different qualities and potential.

When, without preferences, colors join in the dance and embrace forms they give birth to an extraordinary world of expanded realities. In creation, colors, forms, and images cross the boundaries of thinking and sit in the heart to narrate tales of feeling and discovery.

Looking at Your
Finished Paintings

We all know that art is not truth.
Art is a lie that makes us realize truth.

PICASSO

During the first year of my creative process, I painted a man and a woman embracing. The painting seemed to come out of me like magic. It painted itself. The tones, colors, and proportions were pleasing and harmonious; the two bodies were flowing into each other with perfect ease. I was in awe at what had happened. I loved to look at the painting and its intricacies. I decided to hang it in the hallway of my two-bedroom apartment in Paris.

Every time I passed the picture, I couldn't help looking at it. I soon noticed that each time I looked, I thought about it. I was brought into the past, into that fixed point in time long gone. That affected the thrust of my process and confused it. When I finally took down the painting and stored it in my closet, I felt great release. I was free again to go forward and explore. I realized that for a couple of weeks I had been carrying the burden of the past. That day, I understood how important it is to let go of what was done, and I put myself fully into the hands of the creative process. The creative process has intelligence. When something has been painted, it knows it. It moves from that place, and exploration continues without having to think about it or going back.

Every painting is part of an inner movement, a *link in a cycle.* If what has been done is singled out and made important, the cycle is broken. One function of creativity is to challenge self-consciousness and its demands. If the painting is used for esthetic or analytical reasons, the purpose is defeated. Yet the mind with its understanding has its place. I do recommend that paintings be looked at every so often, but in chronological order so as to see the movement of the creative journey. I look at my paintings every few months or every year after they have been put on slides. I let my intuition sense the movement of my process. I do not interpret or search for meaning. I listen to my intuition just as I do in the painting process. I am often overwhelmed by the beauty of the intelligence I discover, although it often takes days of sensing openly before insights or realization arise.

It is important to learn how to look at paintings so the thinking mind does not take over with its assumptions and desires. Insights will be born on their own when the painter witnesses without prejudices the inner journey that has taken place. The desire to look at a painting after it is finished can feel very natural. The mind wants to understand what happened, to read meaning in it, to rejoice at the accomplishment, and to imagine how people will react. There is nothing wrong with that, but it has consequences. To study your painting may bring you back in your head and break the beautiful connection you have developed between you and your process. The temptation to control the next painting may arise and cause creative blocks. Keeping in mind the next blank canvas rather than your last work is a dynamic way of keeping creation flowing.

The desire to study your paintings comes from two assumptions: One, that the doing is not enough in itself, and two, that what the spontaneous painting has expressed can be understood just by looking at it. Of course the content of a painting can be understood on one level, but the deeper connections that pure creativity establish have to work their way through organically and in their own time. To look at or study a painting risks slowing your process and stopping insights. Ultimately, it is a personal decision. You have to see what serves you most and ask what you want out of painting.

Professional artists need to dwell between these parameters protecting their freedom as much as possible. I often recommend that they separate their professional art from their explorative art and see what happens. This way, they will have one place with total freedom. Then, they can watch how these two places spontaneously intermingle.

Showing
Your Paintings

There is an exquisite quality in the heart. When the heart finds beauty, it does not hold it for itself; it shares it with others. The first reaction is to want to show your painting to others and watch their delight. The beauty is truly there, vibrant and giving. I see so much of it in my workshops that I have almost stopped going to museums.

Wanting to show what you love is a very natural and healthy desire. The trouble is that others might not be tuned into that deep level of receptivity. It is like a lover's love that sees depths, integrity, and generosity in the other and love them for all that beauty. A passerby might see only the clothes on their backs or what they eat or do for a living. Receiving such a narrow response when you share your pictures could generate creative blocks.

The other danger, of course, is to have a swollen ego. Painters might begin to think that they have painted that painting on their own. They might disremember where it came from, ignoring the sacred source. *Truly, who is the painter?* A misconception could possibly damage the painters lifeline to inspiration.

Be careful if and when and to whom you show your paintings. The question is, what would serve most your Creative Quest, the quest in the depths of your self? Beauty needs an open heart to be received. Not every heart is ready to receive it.

Point Zero
for All Art
Forms

hether recognized or not, the urge to create inhabits everyone. It is part of our makeup. That urge to create can manifest in an unlimited number of forms and mediums, each specifically attuned to its creator. Some feel the pull to writing, some to playing music, dancing, sculpting, gardening, or endless other art forms.

Regardless of the medium, the purpose of creation is always to find one's true voice, an original way to feel and express. True creation is a pure manifestation of who we are and what we perceive at all levels of being. The voice of creation cannot be confused with any other voice; it is molded to the person, unique in its expression. To reach the place of creation, we need to meet Point Zero and become acquainted with it. If we want to continue creating, we have to develop a relationship with it and not to be at the mercy of a scarce and capricious inspiration.

Point Zero has the amazing quality of finding you wherever you are on the map of your consciousness and bringing you back home. Whether you are partially engaged in your work or wandering aimlessly, lost in expectations and beliefs, Point Zero pulls you back to the center of your being and brings your attention to the essential in creation. When you are creating from only a fragment of your self,

Point Zero demands that you gather together all the pieces and respond from your whole being.

How does Point Zero work?

Point Zero has the extraordinary power and wisdom of that which offers no resistance. Point Zero opens a path of acceptance by opening its arms to the enemy—the demands and avoidances of your mind—and welcoming it. Point Zero disarms it. By following the enemy to its hidden place, to its loot, Point Zero releases the pressure of secrets and fears. The great miracle of creation happens: Everything returns to its source; no struggle, no deceit, no denial can withhold the beauty of that acceptance. Point Zero is the place that exists before manipulation, belief, repression, and preference take over.

How do you go to Point Zero?

By asking questions that lead you to the path of no resistance and no preference. On that path, frictions and demands that blocked your way dissolve; the mind-made barriers fall on their own, and true life energy begs you to use it. When the questions directly challenge the judgments, no limits are left to your creation. Creativity can follow intuition without the pressure of product and without guilt or regret. The passageway to the heart is suddenly reopened, and the universal creative energy has room to flow and mold forms into new shapes. The force of the universal impregnates the fertile womb of the creator. It does not matter which medium you use. The principles of creativity and its ways of working are the same, and they are universal.

APPENDIX

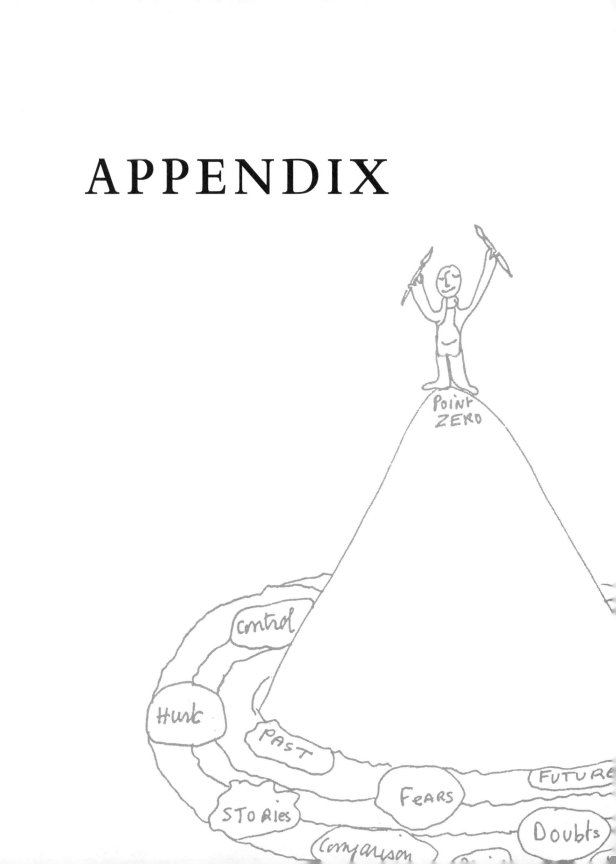

Brushes, Paint, and Paper

The painting process is not tied to certain materials. Many different types of paint will work. *What is important is how you do it.*

I like to use easy-to-spread, quick-drying paint. Tempera paints lend themselves well to the painting process. They should be of good quality. They are not costly and can free you from the fear of wasting precious materials. If you want a more concentrated pigment, you can use gouache, a more expensive paint. Any other paints will work as long as they allow you to be spontaneous and to paint as fast as you need. If you are already used to other paints, you can keep using them, though it could be an interesting experiment to try tempera for a while to see if it affects your inspiration.

You need at least six basic colors to get started: white, red, blue, green, yellow, and black. You can mix these colors to make some more. If you want to buy six more colors, you can get orange, brown, violet, peach, turquoise, and magenta.

I recommend using good brushes, which, if well taken care of, can last twenty years. I use Isabey 6227z-2 watercolor brushes. They are drop-shape pointed brushes, known as round brushes. An assortment of three or four brushes is good to have. Most quality brushes come in different sizes. Good sizes to start with are #000,

#2, and #3. The Loew-Cornell standard quality synthetic brushes also work well—#6, #10, #14, 7000 series round—as well as Loew-Cornell 7350-1-liner (less expensive). Or you can try Utrecht #6 and #12. Of course you can use any other watercolor brush that will hold enough paint and will follow your gesture well.

I choose to paint on paper. You can find many different qualities of paper at your local art store. The paper should not to be too grainy or too smooth. You want to avoid paper that absorbs too much paint or not enough. 80 Vellum bristol paper works well. You can find it in printing paper suppliers places, and it is reasonably priced. A good size is 26 x 20 or 22 x 28. (Other good brands are Springhill and Wasau Exact.)

All of these supplies are available at reasonable prices through **Art Innovations,** a mail-order company. Visit their website at artinnovations.com or call 1-800-789-9621 or e-mail to artinnovations@earthlink.net. Other mail-order companies with reasonably priced art supplies include **Nasco** (1-800-558-9595 or 920-563-2446) and **Sax Arts and Crafts** (1-800-558-6696). Call to request a catalog.

Contact Information

The Point Zero method described in this book is now *exclusively* taught under the name Michele Cassou Painting Workshops. The Painting Experience Studio mentioned in her book *Life, Paint and Passion* has been closed for a few years. The co-authors of the book have dissolved their partnership and are presently following their own directions and different philosophies.

To receive information on painting workshops offered, for a list of books, audios, and videotapes, or to be put on a mailing list, please contact:

Michele Cassou Painting Workshops
369-B Third Street PM B 279
San Rafael, CA 94901
Tel. (415) 721-3812 or (415) 459-4829
Fax: (415) 459-4829
Website: www.pointzeropainting.com
E-mail: ptzeropainting@aol.com

Acknowledgments

I want to give my warmest heartfelt thanks and immense gratitude to Jeremy Tarcher. It has been a privilege and a joy to work closely with him. Jeremy has played a key part in the birth and unfoldment of this book, helping it grow with his unending support, enthusiasm, and depth of understanding. I extend my thanks to Tarcher/Putnam for publishing *Point Zero* and to Sara Carder for coordinating the project.

I want to thank Sue Mann, my first editor, who has been so dedicated to correct my English language without taking my voice away. I want to thank Carol Rosenberg for a caring and excellent job in doing the second editing. I want to thank my dear friend and colleague Carol Levow for her loving support during the writing of this book and Samantha Newman for her deep generosity transcribing dozens of audiotapes. I also want to thank Judy Garland, Barbara Rivkin, Margrit Haeberlin, George and Natalia Rosenfeld, Diane Hullet, Richard Buell, my brother Georges Cassou, Denise and Rudy Meltnizer, Tania Heyman, Gloria Kalisher, and Clara Antonietti for their love and support during this last year, as well as Maria Fortin of the Mabel Dodge Luhan House. I extend my loving gratefulness to all my students for teaching me the many things I learned and I am still learning while with them, inspiring me to always discover more depths to creativity and allowing me to be part of their Creative Quest. And last but not least, I thank the Creative Spirit that has given me my greatest joys.

About the Author

MICHELE CASSOU was born and raised in southern France. She started to draw and paint at five years old. As a young adult, she moved to Paris, where she studied law, literature, and art. There she painted with children for more than three years in a free expression studio, away from all traditional rules and concepts about art and learned to understand the amazing life-changing potential of creation.

As a young woman, Michele moved to Canada, where she continued to paint intensely while teaching her method of "free expression" at Ottawa University. Through observation and experimentation, she began her lifelong search for the understanding of the creative process and how to share it with others. A unique method grew out of her many years of just painting for herself and helping her students dive into the creative process. In 1978 she moved to California where she opened her own painting studio and began teaching classes and workshops.

A passionate artist, Michele has painted over 5,000 paintings and has made videos of her work. She is known internationally for her groundbreaking work in exploring the spiritual dimensions of the creative process. Presently she teaches the Point Zero method under the name *Michele Cassou Painting Workshops*. She conducts workshops in the San Francisco area, at the Esalen Institute in Big Sur, at the New York Open Center, at the Mabel Dodge Luhan House in Taos, and at various other locales in the United States and Europe. She lives in San Rafael, California.